T0354308

GUIDEBOOK

to

HISTORIC HOUSES

and

GARDENS

in

NEW ENGLAND

GUIDEBOOK

to

HISTORIC HOUSES
and
GARDENS
in
NEW ENGLAND

71 Sites from
the Hudson Valley East

Willit Mason

⬤iUniverse®

GUIDEBOOK OF HISTORIC HOUSES AND GARDENS IN NEW ENGLAND
71 SITES FROM THE HUDSON VALLEY EAST

iUniverse books may be ordered through booksellers or by contacting:

iUniverse
1663 Liberty Drive
Bloomington, IN 47403
www.iuniverse.com
1-800-Authors (1-800-288-4677)

Because of the dynamic nature of the Internet, any web addresses or links contained in this book may have changed since publication and may no longer be valid. The views expressed in this work are solely those of the author and do not necessarily reflect the views of the publisher, and the publisher hereby disclaims any responsibility for them.

Any people depicted in stock imagery provided by Thinkstock are models, and such images are being used for illustrative purposes only. Certain stock imagery © Thinkstock.

ISBN: 978-1-5320-2540-2 (sc)
ISBN: 978-1-5320-2541-9 (e)

Library of Congress Control Number: 2017910330

Print information available on the last page.

iUniverse rev. date: 07/13/2017

DEDICATION

For Keteer, Elizabeth, Willie, Corey, Charlie and John - my favorites!

INTRODUCTION

In the summer of 2015, after 45 years, I retired from the practice of medicine. In celebration, my wife and I decided to take a trip to the Berkshires and the Hudson Valley region of New York on our way to Minnesota. The choice of these two areas was driven not only by their natural beauty but also by the number of historic estates and gardens that lie along the Hudson River and amongst the hills of the Berkshires.

Over the years I have admired these "summer retreats" since as a college student in the late 70's, I painted the barn at "Naumkeag" in Stockbridge, Massachusetts. Over the years I have had occasion to visit other estates in New England and other regions of the country. More recently I served on the board of Blithewold Mansion and Gardens in Bristol, Rhode Island. Each visit has captured me in different ways whether it be the scenic views, architecture of the houses, gardens and landscape architecture or collections of art. As we have learned from "Downton Abbey", every house has its own personal story and most of its original owners have made significant contributions to American history as well as its cultural and economic growth.

In preparation for our trip, I was unable to find a guidebook which would give the highlights of both the house and gardens, define their geographic context and summarize their particular strengths. For example, some locations might offer a terrific horticultural experience but have less historical interest or vice versa. The traveler and his or her companion should have a good idea of what they are going to experience before driving 45 miles to visit. Some people like gardens, others history, and others just like to take in the view. These estates potentially will allow you to enjoy all these aspects, but some do it better than others.

The title of this book "Historic Houses and Gardens in New England" implies that all the houses are historic and associated with significant gardens. This is not totally accurate since there are gardens without houses in this book. Where this is the case, my hope is that the garden or house is significant enough to justify considering a visit given its proximity to other estates in a given area. At the end of each discussion of a house or garden, I will attempt to summarize the attributes of each site so that the traveler can make a more informed choice regarding a visit according to their mood, interest and in some sites their physical capabilities (some sites entail a great deal of walking). I purposely do not attempt to render judgments about the quality of sites as I am not an expert in horticulture, garden and landscape design or architecture, and for most, such judgments can be very personal. However, in situations where I did not feel this excitement, the site was not included in the book.

This book is organized by region, and a region may include sites from more than one state. Hopefully, the regional approach will help you avoid driving long distances from site to site. While you are visiting, you may want to find time to take advantage of New England's wealth of history, cultural activity and geography.

Finally, timing is everything in New England, and the seasons need to be considered in planning a tour. Many of the houses are open year-round, although many do close at the New Year and do not open until April or May. The gardens are always in transition, and their peak is frequently an individual preference. Generally, the gardens begin to see activity in April or early May with the blooming of daffodils and begin to become dormant in early October with the first frost. There may be a 2 to 3 week variation depending on the severity of the winter and whether your trip is to southern or northern New England. It is a good idea to check the website of each garden not only for seasonal openings and closings, but also for specific information regarding tours or special events.

TABLE OF CONTENTS

RHODE ISLAND

Rhode Island is the smallest state in the U.S., and therefore the sites in this section are usually within an hour driving time of one another. Most of the houses and gardens are located in Newport or in nearby maritime towns. The Newport houses were built in the "Gilded Age" on large and impressive estates with sweeping lawns, magnificent trees and grounds and large formal gardens (The Elms, Rough Point, Rosecliff and The Breakers). The exception is Whitehorne House, which was built after the Revolutionary War and is located in the old part of Newport near the wharves and harbor.

Another "Gilded Age" estate, Blithewold is located north of Newport and lies outside of Bristol Harbor. Nearby is Green Animals Topiary Garden which, like Blithewold, has views of Narragansett Bay and extensive gardens. However, the house is smaller, simpler, and not meant to impress.

Shakespeare's Head Garden is located at the northernmost aspect of Narragansett Bay and is a city garden in Providence. This is the only garden in Rhode Island in which the house is not open to the public.

NOTE: INFORMATION REGARDING DAYS AND HOURS OF OPERATION AS WELL AS FEES AT EACH SITE ARE SUBJECT TO CHANGE AND IT IS BEST TO PHONE OR CHECK THE WEBSITE OF EACH LOCATION FOR UP TO DATE INFORMATION.

Rhode Island

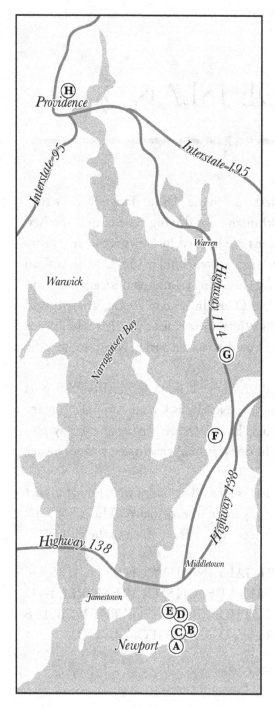

(A) Rough Point
680 Bellevue Ave, Newport, RI

(B) The Breakers
44 Ochre Point Ave, Newport, RI

(C) Rosecliff
548 Bellevue Ave, Newport, RI

(D) The Elms
367 Bellevue Ave, Newport, RI

(E) Whitehorne House
416 Thames St, Newport, RI

(F) Green Animals
380 Cory's Ln, Portsmouth, RI

(G) Blithewold
101 Ferry Rd, Bristol, RI

(H) Shakespeare's Head Garden
21 Meeting St, Providence, RI

ROUGH POINT

680 Bellevue Avenue, Newport, RI 02840
Website: www.newportrestoration.org
Phone: 401-847-8344
Season: Early April to early November-
Hours and Days of Operation: Variable from month to month-check website
    or call
House Tours: Guided and self-guided tours are available - check website for
    times
Entry Fees: Guided Tours: $25 Adult/ Children under 12 free; Self Guided
    Tours: $10 Adult

    Construction of Rough Point started in 1887 and was commissioned by Frederick W. Vanderbilt, the sixth son of William. At the time of its construction, it was the largest house in Newport, RI and occupied a site of approximately 11 acres which overlooked the craggy rocks and cliffs at the end of Aquidneck Island. Built in the English Manorial style, it was furnished to project the mood of an English country house. The grounds and gardens were designed by the firm of F.L. and J.C. Olmsted. Apparently, life in Newport did not agree with Mr. Vanderbilt, and he sold the house in 1906 to the Leeds family, who sold the house to James Duke in 1922. Mr. Duke was a very wealthy man who owned and founded the American Tobacco Company as well as Duke Energy. He and his wife had spent summers in Newport previously as renters. When Rough Point became available, he purchased it for $375,000. From 1922 to 1924, the house was renovated and substantially enlarged. In 1924, the Dukes and their 12-year-old daughter moved into the house. Unfortunately, Mr.

Duke only had one year to enjoy the house as he died in 1925 at age 68, leaving his fortune and Rough Point to his daughter, Doris. Doris spent her teenage years in Newport but lost interest when in 1935, she married James Cromwell. While married, she spent years traveling around the world and finding other nests to settle into.

After the hurricane of 1938, her mother also became less interested in Rough Point, and in the 1950's, had all the furnishings removed to storage. In the late 1950's, after two failed marriages and the loss of a premature baby, Doris's interest in Newport was rekindled, and from 1958 to 1962, she furnished the house with many of its original contents, as well as adding her own choice of art and antiques. Doris moved back in 1962, and subsequently spent some of her time from May to November in Newport. During that period, having become very involved with the preservation of historic Newport, she was able to save historic houses from the wrecking balls, and subsequently restore and modernize them so they could be rented or sold. Doris died in 1993, leaving a fortune of over $1 billion that was used to fund The Doris Duke Charitable Foundation. This foundation, among many other things, supports the house museums at Rough Point and Whitehorne as well as the 70 historic houses that she successfully saved in Newport.

Guided tours of Rough Point run hourly April through October, and allow the visitor to view Doris Duke's various collections which include Flemish tapestries, French furniture and European art such as works by Renoir, Van Dyck, Gainsborough and Palma il Vecchio. Visitors are shown the first floor rooms with their dramatic views of the ocean. Tours of the second floor are limited to Doris's bed chamber and a gallery for special exhibits. When the 75-minute house tour ends, the visitor is provided a map explaining the house and gardens and invited to wander the 11-acre grounds and gardens designed by the Olmsted Brothers over 100 years ago. Closest to the house and at the south end of the property, there is the kitchen garden which is an enclosed vegetable and flower cutting garden. Visitors are then naturally drawn over the rolling lawn behind the house to the ocean's edge, with its rock outcroppings and hollows. The rocks are planted with Alpine plants, evergreens and beach roses. At the northern edge of the property and away from the ocean, there is a formal garden enclosed by a privet hedge and not visible from the house. Originally a cutting garden, it now includes a combination of perennials, annuals, grasses and bulbs that provide an explosion of textures and colors all summer. A 13 bay rose arbor borders the formal garden and ends at a stone sculpture.

Rough Point

■ THE BREAKERS

44 Ochre Point Avenue, Newport, RI 02840
Website: www.newportmansions.org
Telephone: 401-847-1000
Season: Open year round except Christmas and Thanksgiving
Hours of Operation: Varies by season - check the website or telephone
Day of Tours: Variable - Check the website
Entry Fees: Packages are available - check the website or call

Newport, RI is located on Aquidneck Island and prior to the Revolutionary War, was one of the busiest ports in America with its participation in the "Triangle Trade" (rum for slaves and molasses). In the early 1800's, the slave trade was prohibited in the United States, and Newport slowly transformed from a rich and thriving port to a summer community for wealthy Southerners who sought relief from the heat of the South by taking advantage of the cooling breezes of Newport's seacoast. After the Civil War, rapid industrialization with its associated wealth fueled the "Gilded Age", and Newport was again transformed from the playground of rich Southerners (now impoverished by the Civil War) to the showplace of rich Northern industrialists. Three of the five sons of William Henry Vanderbilt were part of this wave, and in the 1890's, each built a "summer cottage". Frederick built Rough Point, then decided he did not like Newport and moved to Hyde Park, NY. William and his wife built Marble House, possibly the most expensive house built in Newport ($11 million) and Cornelius II built "The Breakers," the largest house ever built in Newport, encompassing 138,000 square feet with 70 rooms and 300 windows.

Cornelius II (1843-1899) was the oldest son of William Henry Vanderbilt (1821-1885) and the favorite grandson of Cornelius, "The Commodore", Vanderbilt (1794-1877). "The Commodore" originated the Vanderbilt fortune first by maritime shipping and then with the development of the largest railroad system in America, the New York Central. The "Commodore's son", William Henry, doubled his father's fortune from 1877 until his death in 1885. William's fortune was then left to eight surviving children who proceeded to spend their windfall by building large estates in the Northern United States.

Cornelius II and William Jr. took over the control of the New York Central, but left the management of daily operations to hired hands, leaving them time to pursue other interests. In 1867, Cornelius married Alice Gwynne whom he had met teaching Sunday School, and they proceeded to have seven children. In 1885, they purchased a large wooden house on the current site of the present day Breakers for $450,000 and summered there until it burned down in 1892. Subsequently, they hired Richard Morris Hunt (the Vanderbilt architect of the Breakers, Marble House, Biltmore, and the Metropolitan Museum of Art) to build a fireproof house that would reflect the importance of the Vanderbilt family as an economic and social force in American life. Hunt chose to design an Italian Renaissance palace with all the modern amenities. Despite its size and ornateness, it took only two years to complete and furnish (his brother WIlliam's house, Marble House, took four years). All the furnishings and much of the interior of the first-floor ornamentation were produced in France by Jules Allard and shipped to Newport. The first floor was palatial with gilded rooms centered by a great hall. The family rooms on the second and third floor were designed by Ogden Codman (see The Mount and Kykuit) to be more comfortable and much less ornate. The third and fourth floors also held bedrooms for the 40 house servants required to run the house.

The Breakers was completed in 1895. Unfortunately, Cornelius had little time to enjoy the house, because he had a severe stroke in 1896 and in 1899, he died. His wife, Alice, continued to live there until her death in 1934, when her daughter, Gladys, who lived abroad and was married to a Hungarian count, inherited it. In 1948, Gladys opened the ground floor to the public for an entrance fee that was given to the Preservation Society of Newport County and continued to use the third and fourth floors. Gladys died in 1965, and in 1972 the house was sold to the Preservation Society for $399,997.

The Breakers is open daily year-round. Visitors can choose from two audio tours of the first and second floors. One of the tours is geared toward children. There are no specific tours of the 13 acres of grounds which look over the cliffs, the "Cliff Walk" of Newport, and onto the Atlantic Ocean. The grounds were designed by James and Ernest Bowditch. The perimeter of the property is enclosed by a 12-foot iron fence, and inside the fence are rhododendrons and pathways planted with European beeches and false cypresses. Behind the house is large terrace that looks down a long lawn to the ocean beyond. Sunken gardens enclosed by balustrades and planted with annuals are located on the north and south side of the house.

Ocean side of the Breakers
Courtesy of Gavin Ashworth and The Preservation
Society of Newport County

ROSECLIFF

548 Bellevue Avenue, Newport, RI 02840
Website: www.newportmansions.org
Phone: 401-847-1000
Season: Daily year-round except Thanksgiving and Christmas
Hours and days of operation: Variable by season - check website or phone for details
Entry fees: Phone or check website as various packages available

Like many of the great houses in Newport, Rhode Island, Rosecliff is located on Bellevue Avenue and looks over rocky cliffs and the Atlantic beyond. The house, designed by Stanford White, was built of white terra cotta but resembles white marble. It was modeled after the Grand Trianon, the garden retreat of Louis XIV, and it was completed in 1902, reportedly for $2.5 million ($70 million today). It had nine bedrooms and eight bathrooms on the second floor and the largest ballroom in Newport.

Theresa "Tessie" Oelrichs made it all happen. Tessie was the daughter of an Irish immigrant who discovered the Comstock Lode in Nevada, the largest silver discovery in history of the United States. She met her husband, Hermann, while playing tennis at the Newport Casino, and in 1891 they bought the property on which Rosecliff now stands. Hermann was a great athlete, sportsman and also quite rich, as he was the American agent for his family's North German Lloyd Shipping Line. Tessie, however, was the driving force in the marriage and belonged to the Newport Triumvirate. This group of women made up of Tessie, Alva Vanderbilt and Mamie Fish, displaced Mrs. Astor as the arbiters of Newport society from 1900 to World War I. Under their leadership, the pace and extravagance of the Newport social scene accelerated. Reportedly, it was not unusual for the "lady of the house" to budget $500,000 ($15 million today) to cover the cost of social activities for the summer.

The excesses of this time were all part of the "Gilded Age" which was fueled by the Industrial Revolution, technological innovations, the advent of railroads and cheap labor provided by immigration. The "Gilded Age" began after the Civil War and ended with the initiation of the income tax in 1913 and the ability of the servant class to find better paying jobs in a booming economy after World War I. Hermann Oelrichs died of a heart attack in 1906. In the early 1920's, Tessie was blinded in one eye in a household accident and soon after suffered a mental breakdown. Her health deteriorated, and in 1926, she died and left the house to her son Hermann Jr. who was not interested in maintaining the social pace of his mother. Rather than dancing, he used the ballroom for roller skating and ping pong. He was a great friend of Cole Porter's who reportedly spent many summers at Rosecliff.

In 1940, Hermann sold the mansion to singer and actress Gertrude Niesen for $21,000. Unfamiliar with Newport winters, she left the house unwinterized and during the winter, the pipes froze and burst creating tremendous damage to the house. Rosecliff was then bought by Ray Allen Van Clief who had the house restored, but was killed in an automobile accident before he could move in. In the late 1940's, J. Edgar Monroe of New Orleans purchased the house, and he and his wife lived there until 1971, when they gave the house and its furnishings to the Preservation Society of Newport County along with an endowment for its maintenance.

The grounds of Rosecliff are beautiful with a sweeping lawn and mature beech trees lining a gravel driveway up to the house. The entrance to the house features a marble terrace divided by boxwood hedges and interspersed with statuary. A formal garden with a central fountain and gravel path is located at the front of the house. To the right of the house is the rose garden. The Oelrichs had purchased the property and the original house from George Bancroft. An historian, diplomat, Secretary of the Navy and one of the founders of the Naval War College, Bancroft was an avid horticulturalist who cultivated over 500 species of roses on this property which he had named "Roseclyffe". Behind the house is another terrace and a circular pool with a central fountain. Best of all, looking over the sweeping lawn, is a spectacular view of the Atlantic Ocean.

Rosecliff Fountain-Courtesy of The Preservation Society of Newport County

THE ELMS

367 Bellevue Avenue, Newport, RI 02840
Website: www.newportmansions.org
Phone: 1-401-847-1000
Season: Year-round except Thanksgiving and Christmas
Hours and days of operation: Varies by season - Check website or call
Entry fees: Various ticket packages are available - check website or call

One of the largest houses in Newport, the Elms, was built by Edward Julius Berwind between 1898-1901 at a cost of $1.4 million (about $42 million today). The son of German immigrants, Berwind was born in Philadelphia in 1848 and after his graduation from the Naval Academy in 1869, he became the naval aide to President Grant. On retiring from the Navy in 1875, he went into the coal business with his brother Charles to form the Berwind White Coal Company. By working with J.P. Morgan, the company became the largest supplier of coal in the United States and the largest owner of coal mines in the world, making Edward a very rich man.

In 1886 Berwind married Herminie Torrey, an American who had spent most of her life in Italy while her father was in the diplomatic service. The couple spent many summers in Newport before deciding to build a "summer cottage" that mimicked the French château D' Asnieres outside of Paris. To accomplish this, the Berwinds created a 10-acre lot by purchasing three less imposing cottages on Bellevue Avenue and tearing them down. They engaged Horace Trumbauer as architect. Trumbauer was a prominent architect of the "Gilded Age" who satisfied his clients by building houses that made a statement regarding their esteemed stature in the world. His houses also were well regarded, because he was able to incorporate all the modern conveniences with great subtlety. The ornate interior was designed by Allard and Sons of Paris, the interior designer of the Breakers. Finished in 1901, the 60,000 square foot mansion had all the modern conveniences such as electricity, an elevator and modern plumbing.

The Berwinds never had children, but they were devoted to their four nieces who occupied four of the seven bedrooms on the second floor. The top floor accommodated the 40 servants required to keep the house running efficiently. Herminie died in 1922 at the age of 62, and Edward died in 1936 at the age of 88. At his wife's death, he asked his sister Julia to take over as hostess, and she maintained this role until 1961. At her death, the house along with its contents was sold and was at risk of being torn down to make room for a shopping center. Fortunately, with its purchase in 1962, the Preservation Society of Newport saved the house and then opened the house to the public.

The rear of the house overlooks a sloping lawn of several acres. The marble terrace that lies between the house and lawn is adorned with works from the Berwinds's collection of classical sculptures. Interspersed over the lawn are mature specimen trees including beeches, elms and chestnuts, many of which are well marked. At the far end of the lawn is a pavilion modeled after Versailles and a sunken Classical Revival garden. Next to the garden there is a magnificent stable and carriage house, part of which has recently been adaptively restored into living and work space for visiting scholars. Although the mansion does not border the ocean, the view from the house and terraces offers a distant glimpse of Newport Harbor.

Audio tours of the house are available but not of the garden. The tour is well down and gives the visitor a sense of the family and what it was like to live or work at the Elms. The tour includes the public areas of the first floor, the living quarters of the second floor and the basement kitchen. A separate guided "Servant Life Tour" takes visitors to the staff working areas in the basement and sub-basement, including the boiler room, coal room and laundry rooms, as well as the third floor staff living quarters and the roof. Although many of the furnishings were sold at the death of the last Berwind, many of the family's collections of furniture, Renaissance Ceramics, 18th century French and Venetian Paintings and Oriental jade have been recovered and are on display.

Elms Garden Facade
Courtesy of Gavin Ashworth and The Preservation
Society of Newport County

WHITEHORNE HOUSE

416 Thames Street, Newport, RI. 02840
Website: www.newportrestoration.org
Phone: 401-847-2448
Season: See Website-closed in 2017
Hours and Dates of Operation: see Website
Entry Fees: see Website

Before the Revolutionary War, Newport, Rhode Island was the fifth largest city in the American colonies and the third largest port. Its merchants were involved with the Triangle Trade - trading rum for slaves, molasses and mahogany. Samuel Whitehorne's father was involved in this trade and his two sons followed in his footsteps. During the Revolutionary War, Newport was occupied by British soldiers, and its commerce was destroyed as half the population of Newport fled. After the war, the city never fully returned to its dominance as an economic force.

Despite the devastation of the economy, Samuel Whitehorne Jr. (1779-1844) and his brother John were exceptions. They continued on in the shipping business and other enterprises such as banking. Their success allowed Samuel Jr. to build a Federal style mansion in 1811, a block away from the family homestead which was the site of the family distillery. The mansion was located on Thames Street and overlooked the docks and warehouses of Newport Harbor. Samuel and his wife occupied the house until 1843, when Samuel lost two of his ships at sea and suffered severe financial difficulties.

After Samuel's death in 1844, the house was owned by mill owners whose mills had been built along Thames Street next to the harbor. With the abolition of the slave trade in 1808, the flow of slave importation was significantly reduced, and cotton and its production became a more important part of Newport's economy. Eventually, cotton production in Newport tapered off, and the 20th century brought harder times to the city. In the early 20th century, the front of Whitehorne house was added onto to create a storefront. The remainder of the house was used as a boarding house.

In 1969, the Newport Restoration Foundation purchased the house and restored the house and gardens to their former grandeur. Because of its size, Doris Duke (see Rough Point) chose it to be a museum for her collection of 18th century Newport and Rhode Island furniture.

The mansion is generally open on Thursday, Friday and Saturday in the summer months (although closed in the 2017 season), and the gardens are open daily from dawn to dusk. Tours of the house focus primarily on the antiques, and both the self-guided and guided tours serve as primers to understanding the differences between cabinetmakers of the major furniture producers in New York, Boston and Philadelphia. The collection features furniture designed and built by the Townsend and Goddard families and Benjamin Baker - possibly the greatest furniture makers in American history. Even for visitors without an interest in American antiques, the house itself is well worth seeing and has been beautifully restored. Despite its location on the busiest street in Newport, the mansion has a significant terraced garden that ascends the hill behind the house and can be entered through two garden gates. Restored in the last ten years, the garden is typical of the Federal style period. Gravel paths with catmint borders define the flower beds. Fruit trees and a white picket fence separate this garden oasis from the bustling streets of the city.

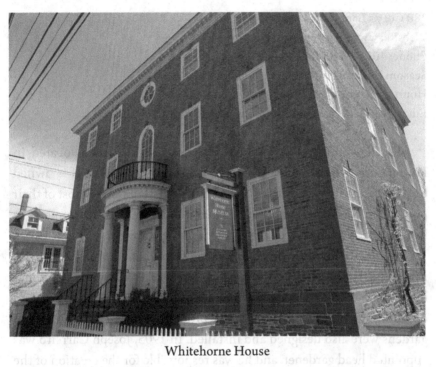

Whitehorne House

GREEN ANIMALS TOPIARY GARDEN

380 Cory's Lane, Portsmouth, RI 02871
Website: www.newportmansions.org
Phone: 401-847-1000
Season: End of May to end of October
Hours and days of operation: Daily from 1 -5 pm
Entry Fees: Check website or phone as packages are available

Green Animals is the name of a house and garden located in Portsmouth, Rhode Island overlooking Narragansett Bay. It is owned by the Preservation Society of Newport County but unlike most of their properties, the scale is more modest and more human. It is unique in having one of the finest topiary gardens in the country.

In 1877, Thomas Brayton, a businessman from Fall River, Massachusetts purchased the farm as a retreat to escape the summer heat of the city. The 7 acre farm consisted of a clapboard house and outbuildings. The farm continued to produce its own food, but formal gardens were also designed and installed. In 1905, Joseph Carreiro was appointed head gardener, and he was responsible for the creation of the formal gardens and the topiary. Joseph continued with this job until his death in 1945, at which time his son-in-law took over the job until 1985. Over 80 topiaries are spread throughout several different formal gardens. Some are very subtle such as a basket or small duck, but others are more obvious such as the elephant or giraffe. The gardens are well-maintained, and the creation of new topiary continues on.

After Brayton's death, his daughter, Alice, inherited the house and made it her full-time residence in 1940 and remained there until her death in 1972. She left Green Animals to the Preservation Society of Newport County and the house and garden are open to the public. Most of the furnishings are Victorian and belonged to Alice. There is also an interesting collection of dollhouses and other antique toys which children should enjoy seeing. The view from the front porch with its rocking chairs allows you to look down the back lawn through mature trees (tulips, green ash, larch, sycamore maple, and horse chestnut) onto Narragansett Bay. The ability to rock on the porch and enjoy the view on a hot summer afternoon makes the trip worthwhile. The gardens and the house are icing on the cake.

Garden at Green Animals
Courtesy of Richard Cheek and The Preservation
Society of Newport County

BLITHEWOLD MANSION, GARDENS & ARBORETUM

101 Ferry Road, Bristol, RI 02809
Web site:www.blithewold.org
Phone: 401-253-2707
Season: April 1-October 15 and late November thru January 1rst
Hours and days of operation: Tuesday-Saturday, 10-4 PM and Sunday, 10-3 PM
Days of House Tours: Self Guided Tours Daily and Guided on Wednesday at
    1 Pm
Entry Fees: $14 for adults and $26 for families

On September 20th,1882 Augustus Van Wickle and Bessie Pardee were married before 800 guests in a grand and festive ceremony in Hazleton, Pennsylvania. This marriage brought together two families that controlled much of the coal production of Pennsylvania and its supporting industries such as banking, iron, lumber and railroads. At a time when the eastern United States was experiencing tremendous industrial growth, coal was the major source of energy.

Having graduated from Brown University in 1882, Augustus succeeded his father at his death in 1892 as president of the family business and went on to increase the firm's size and profitability. His success allowed him to search for a summer retreat, and in 1893, he visited a college friend in Rhode Island for that purpose. This ended up being an expensive weekend. Not only did he purchase a 78 foot steam yacht from the Herreshoff Boat Yard in Bristol, Rhode Island, but his host showed him a 70 acre acre farm in Bristol that overlooked Narragansett Bay and featured lovely mature gardens, rare specimens of trees and several greenhouses. Augustus was hooked and a week later, with Bessie's enthusiastic consent, he purchased the farm. Blithewold was born.

The original farm house was moved to serve as a guest house, and the Van Wickles built a Queen Anne style house which was set back from the road and had views overlooking the great lawn onto Narragansett Bay. On the southern end of the property, a golf course with a clubhouse and a dock with a boat house were added. Inheriting her mother's love of gardens and design, Bessie hired John DeWolf, a landscape architect and a member of one of Bristol's oldest families, to help her. DeWolf was a well-respected and published architect who also worked as a designer for the New York City Parks Department. He and Bessie worked together from 1895 until his death in 1913. Together, they created an informal landscape with gravel paths which meander through the property and connect the different gardens. The rose garden with its moongate welcomes visitors to the house where they proceed to the sunken garden, the bosquet with 50,000 daffodils, the enclosed garden with its giant sequoia (the largest on the East Coast), the cutting garden, and the rock and water gardens down on the bay. Pathways allow visitors to view the bay from different perspectives and lead one through many exotic varieties of trees interspersed among the gardens. Because the family kept copious records documenting the gardens, the layout and plant material are very similar to what they were in 1936 when Bessie died.

In the summer of 1896, the family moved into the house and enjoyed all that they had worked and planned so hard for. The house and guest house were full of friends and family, since Bessie had 10 brothers and sisters with families of their own. The gardens matured and the family took advantage of every activity the property offered including swimming, sailing, golf, tennis, music and painting. Augustus's business continued to flourish and in the winter, the family began to seek the warmth of Jekyll Island in Georgia. To facilitate travel to their southern retreat, Augustus commissioned a new 185 foot steam yacht in 1898. That same year, Bessie learned that she was pregnant after desperately trying to have a second child for many years. Unfortunately Augustus never saw his second child born or his new yacht launched. In June of 1898, after enjoying Blithewold for only two years, he was killed in a skeet shooting accident, leaving Bessie with 2 daughters - fifteen year old Marjorie and her infant sister Augustine, named for her father.

Bessie remarried in 1901 and continued to enjoy her summers until 1906 when an electrical fire led to the complete destruction of the house. Because the fire originated in the roof, all the furnishings and many architectural components of the house were saved. Blithewold II was rebuilt in the English Manor Style on the same site, but this time, Bessie chose to build it of stone with a slate roof to limit the chances of another fire. With the the completion of Blithewold II in 1908, the bones of the estate were laid down, and today's Blithewold is basically as it was in 1908. The exception was the loss of the 30 acre golf course sold during the 1920's for financial reasons. The family continued to live there until 1976 when the oldest daughter, Marjorie, died at 93. After her death, the house was turned over to the Heritage Trust of R.I. with an endowment to ensure that the gardens and house remain open to the public in perpetuity.

The house at Blithewold is impressive and unique in that it retains the furnishings, paintings, china, clothes, letters and movies of the Van Wickle family. The presence of these items makes the lives and experiences of the family more palpable and provides an unusually rich window onto the "Gilded Age". This is a house that is welcoming and livable. There are no guided house tours, but there are interpretive cards in every room and docents available to answer questions. Guided tours may be arranged for groups of 10 or more. The setting is dramatic, as the house sits on an 11 acre lawn that slopes down to Narragansett Bay and is surrounded by seven gardens and an arboretum. The trees and shrubs are well marked, and a visit to the garden is enhanced by specimen labels, old photographs and strategically placed docents. The estate is within walking distance of Bristol,an old seaport which has preserved much of its original character dating back to 1680.

Blithewold from the gardens

SHAKESPEARE'S HEAD GARDEN

21 Meeting Street, Providence, RI 02903
Website: http:ppsri.org
Phone: 401-831-7440
Hours of Operation: Dawn to dusk
Tours: None
Entry Fees: None

Located in Providence, Rhode Island and down the hill from Brown University and Rhode Island School of Design, this city garden represents an island of nature and tranquility in a busy, but beautiful and historic city. It is situated behind the John Carter House, built around 1772. The house is not open to the public, but the garden can be entered through a gate to the left of the house and is open from dawn until dusk.

The house is a restored colonial, and until 2015, the headquarters for the Providence Preservation Society. John Carter raised his family of 12 children on the upper two floors. and on the the bottom two floors, he had a print shop. An apprentice of Benjamin Franklin, John not only printed books and stationery from these two floors, but he also published the Providence Gazette (a forerunner of Rhode Island's major newspaper). When Benjamin Franklin became Postmaster, he appointed John "Postmaster of Providence", and the post office was also located in this busy house. The name of this house is Shakespeare's Head because, in the Revolutionary period, the use of illustrations or signs was common as advertisements, and Shakespeare's Head was a good choice given the literary output of the first two floors of the house.

The Carter family owned the house until 1906 and after that, it was so neglected that in the mid 1930's, the city threatened to tear it down. A group of concerned citizens raised money to save the house, and the house and garden were restored in 1937. About the size of a city house lot, the garden was designed by James Graham in a Colonial Revival style. Built on a hill, the upper third of the garden is terraced with trees, shrubs and pathways. Directly behind the house is a leveled area which is squared off and divided into pathways and hexagons which contain flower beds. Throughout the garden, there are benches and mature trees to provide shade. There are no tours of the garden, but maps with plant and tree identification can be obtained across the street at the Old Brick Schoolhouse (the new home of the Providence Preservation Society). From the garden, visitors have a view of the majestic steeple arising from the First Baptist Church of America.

BOSTON AND VICINITY

The Boston Route starts at Cape Cod with two sites: 1) Highfield, with its gardens and house which is available for touring (however, most of the furnishings of the house have been removed, and the house has been modernized to function as a cultural center and large art gallery) and 2) Heritage Museum, primarily a series of gardens with the added benefit of a vintage car museum and a museum exhibiting a private collection of paintings, guns, etc. Closer to Boston, but located west of Route 128 (or 95 N), are the Stevens-Coolidge Reservation in Andover, Codman House in Lincoln, and the Eleanor Cabot Bradley Reservation in Canton. All were country weekend retreats for prominent Bostonians. These houses are available for touring, but on a limited basis. However, the gardens and grounds are open dawn to dusk and offer the traveler a nice break from the crush of traffic around Boston. Garden in the Woods, the home of the New England Wild Flower Society, is also located west of Route 128 (95 N) and features trails of wildflowers but no historic house. Fairsted, the home and office of Olmsted, lies east of Route 128 (95 N) and is therefore closer to the city. Both the house and garden are open on a daily basis. Longfellow House, located in Cambridge, and Adams National Park, located in Quincy, really are urban sites located next to Boston, but both have beautiful gardens and grounds as well as houses dating back to the Revolutionary War which are regularly open for touring. The Gardner Museum is the only site in Boston and was certainly a product of the "Gilded Age," but a very unique one. The museum and garden are open regularly. Finally, Tower Hill Botanical Garden, although geographically an orphan as it is located midway between Boston and the Berkshires and just north of Worcester, is well worth a visit, especially if the next stop is the Berkshires (see Berkshire Section).

INFORMATION REGARDING DAYS AND HOURS OF OPERATION AS WELL AS FEES IN EACH SITE SUMMARY ARE SUBJECT TO CHANGE AND IT IS BEST TO PHONE OR CHECK THE WEBSITE OF EACH LOCATION FOR UP TO DATE INFORMATION!

Boston & Vicinity

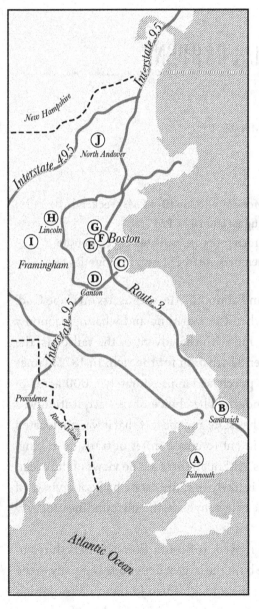

(A) Highfield Hall & Gardens
56 Highfield Dr, Falmouth, MA

(B) Heritage Museums
& Gardens
67 Grove St, Sandwich, MA

(C) Adams National
Historical Park
1250 Hancock St, Quincy, MA

(D) Eleanor Cabot
Bradley Reservation
*2468 B Washington St,
Canton, MA*

(E) Olmsted National
Historic Site
99 Warren St, Brookline, MA

(F) Isabella Stewart
Gardner Museum
25 Evans Way, Boston, MA

(G) Longfellow House
National Historic Site
105 Brattle St, Cambridge, MA

(H) Codman Estate
34 Codman Rd, Lincoln, MA

(I) Garden in the Woods
*184 Hemenway Rd,
Framingham, MA*

(J) Stevens-Coolidge Place
*137 Andover St,
North Andover, MA*

HIGHFIELD HALL & GARDENS

56 Highfield Drive, Falmouth, MA 02540
Website: highfieldhall.org
Phone: 508-495-1878
Season: April 15-October 31
Hours and Days of Operation: Monday - Friday 10-4 PM; Weekends,10-2 PM;
    Friday nights in July and August from 4- 7 PM
House tours are self-guided; Garden tours are available-check website
Entry Fees: $5/ Children and members are free/ Entry to grounds - free

Highfield Hall is located in Falmouth, Massachusetts on Cape Cod. The late 1870's was a time when the maritime and whaling economy on the Cape were declining, and with the advent of the railroads, the Cape was becoming a summer destination for the rich. In 1872, James Madison Beebe (1809-1875) purchased approximately 1,000 acres of fields and woodlands in Falmouth. The choice of this acquisition was atypical because of the size of the estate and the fact that it was not located on the ocean. It was Beebe's intent to create miles of trails for hiking, horseback riding and carriages. Although there are no views of the ocean now, given its site on a hill, it is likely that the estate had good views of Buzzard's Bay, since at the time of its purchase, the surrounding property had many fewer trees.

In 1825 at age 16, Beebe moved to Boston from the Berkshires to seek his fortune. In Boston, he built the largest dry goods company in the United States, and he later partnered with Eben Jordan to form Jordan Marsh, one of the largest department stores in New England. Beebe was also an early founder of the Massachusetts Institute of Technology. In

1866, he sold his dry goods business, and in 1872, began to acquire the Highfield property. Three years later Beebe died, leaving his fortune and property in Falmouth to his six children.

After his death, two houses were built: Highfield by Pearson Beebe, and Tanglewood by J. Arthur Beebe. Tanglewood was torn down in 1977, and Highfield still stands today after escaping the wrecking ball in the 1990's. Believed to have been designed in the Queen Anne Stick style by Peabody and Stearns of Boston, the house was completed in 1878 and measures 17,800 square feet. After a five year restoration period, Highfield opened to the public in 2006. The darker woodwork and colors of the Victorian era have been lightened and modernized, but the basic layout of the house and the architectural details such as floors, paneling, lights and stained glass windows have been preserved. Today, Highfield Hall & Gardens is a unique combination of historic home, restored gardens and vibrant cultural center. Highfield hosts art exhibitions, concerts, festivals, children's programs, garden tours and estate walks. Because of its current usage, the house is only partially furnished and, as a gallery, is open for self guided tours on a daily basis. Information regarding guided tours of the estate is best found on the website.

In the early mid-1960's, the house, gardens, and woods around Highfield were at risk for development but were saved by the efforts of local citizens. The town, with a generous gift from Mr. and Mrs. Josiah Lilly (see Heritage Museum), was able to purchase 337 acres of Beebe Woods, thereby saving much of Highfield's surrounding property. There are 14 miles of hiking trails through these woods which are open to the public and include trails leading over land originally formed by glaciers. Thus, the terrain is often hilly and irregular and contains marshes and ponds. The gardens surrounding the main house were designed by Ernest Bowditch and later by Frederick Law Olmsted. Within the last 10 years they have been restored to reflect their original design and are now open to the public. To the north of the house is a sunken garden and to the west, a shade and sun garden with a central terrace. A path lined with beech trees circles the house and ends in a hollow filled with a variety of rhododendrons.

Courtesy of Highfield Hall and Gardens and Jon Moore

HERITAGE MUSEUMS AND GARDENS

67 Grove Street, Sandwich, MA 02563
Website: www.heritagemuseumsandgardens.org
Season: mid April to mid October - see website for exact dates
Hours and Days of Operation: Daily- 10 AM- 5 PM
Entry Fees: $18 Adults (age 12+) / $8 Children (3-11) / Free-children under 2

The Heritage Museums and Gardens are located in Sandwich, Massachusetts just south of the Cape Cod Canal. Comprising 100 acres, it was originally common land held by the Quakers. A portion was granted to an indigent, widowed mother (Lydia Abbot) in 1672. Lydia's family held the property until 1784. In 1921 Charles Dexter, at the age of 59, purchased the property which was then called Shawme Farm. Charles, a graduate of Brown University, was not only an industrialist as owner of the Beacon Manufacturing Company (the largest producer of cotton blankets in the world), but he also was an accomplished violinist, photographer, yachtsman, and most important, a horticulturalist. Over the next two decades, he pursued his interests by transforming the wooded farm into an estate with gardens, ponds and trails. During this time he became interested in hybridizing rhododendrons, and with his chief gardener, he produced 150,000 - 200,000 seedlings. Many of these were planted in the fields and woods or given away to friends and neighbors. When Charles died in 1943, his wife sold the property. In the mid-1940's, a group of botanists interested in rhododendrons studied Dexter's work, and were so impressed that they named 79 cultivars of rhododendrons after Dexter.

A later owner, Josiah K. Lilly III, an heir to the Eli Lilly pharmaceutical fortune, had a growing collection of antique cars which his own garage could no longer accommodate. Josiah decided to create a museum for two purposes: 1) he wanted a place where he could house and share his collection of antique vintage cars and 2) he wanted to honor his father, also a collector, and share his father's collection with the public. Realizing that a car museum had limited appeal, he thought that combining the museum with gardens would broaden the draw for visitors. In 1966, he bought Shawme Farm, and in 1969, the museum opened.

Visitors to Heritage House may choose from a variety of collections and experiences to suit their own interests. The car museum is housed in a stone Shaker barn and contains about 40 beautiful antique cars, including a two-tone Duesenberg formerly owned by Gary Cooper, and a 1909 White Steam Car which was the first Presidential limousine under President Taft. For children, there is "Hidden Hollow" which includes a 2 acre outdoor discovery and exploration area as well as a giant treehouse. Adjacent to this area is a vintage working carousel located in the museum that houses the collections of Mr. Lilly's father. This collection honors the the evolution of the United States and includes a miniature military collection, paintings, antique guns and carved birds, etc.

The various garden collections include: the daylily garden containing 1200 varieties of lily, the hydrangea collection containing 155 species, a water garden, heather garden, herb garden and so on. The collections are well marked. Trails lead the visitor through woodlands interspersed with 79 different cultivars of the Dexter rhododendrons (the most comprehensive collection in the US). Numerous hiking trails lead over the hilly terrain down to Shawme Pond. For the physically impaired, golf carts are available to facilitate travel around the 100 acres of the gardens and trails.

Wing House at Heritage Museums
Courtesy of Heritage Museums and Gardens-Sandwich, Massachusetts

ADAMS NATIONAL HISTORICAL PARK

1250 Hancock Street, Quincy, MA 02169
Website: www.nps.gov/adam
Phone: 617-770-1175
Season: mid April-mid November-Check Website for exact dates
Hours and Days of Operation: Daily with first tour at 9:15 AM and last tour at 3:15 PM from Visitor Center.
Entry Fees: $10 Adults/ Children under 16-free

Adams National Park is located about 7 miles south of Boston in Quincy, Massachusetts. Quincy is now an urban center, but at the birth of John Adams, the second president of United States, it was farmland. Deacon John Adams, the father of John Adams (1735-1826), was a boot maker in the winter and a farmer in the summer. At his death he left three farm houses and about 200 acres to his three sons. Expected to earn his living by the practice of law and not farming, John inherited one house and 6 acres. Since his brothers had not studied at Harvard as John had, they inherited the bulk of the farmland with the expectation that they would support themselves by farming. However, within the next few years John bought his brothers out, and added to his holdings another 800 acres inherited by his wife Abigail whom he had married in 1764. It was Abigail who ran the farm, while John practiced law, participated in the American Revolution and worked to form a new country.

The tour of the Adams' property starts at the remaining two small farm houses. The city has swallowed up all of the 1000 acres that Abigail farmed, and there no longer is a farm, barns or animals. After the tour of the farm houses, visitors are transported by trolley to Peace field as the second part of the tour.

Peace field was purchased by John Adams in 1788 and became the seat of the Adams family until 1926, when it was turned over to the Adams Memorial Society and eventually the National Park Service. John and Abigail purchased the house while living in Europe where John was helping to negotiate the Paris Peace Treaty of 1783 that ended the American Revolutionary War. He then served in London as the first U.S. minister to England. In Paris and London the Adamses experienced the high life, living in chateaus and palaces. Peace field represented a step up from the old family farmhouse since it was one of the finest houses in Quincy and was surrounded by 75 acres of open land. It had been owned by a loyalist family who owned sugar plantations in the Caribbean, but had been forced to abandon the estate and were anxious to sell given their political status. John and Abigail remembered the house and property from visits many years before, but did not have the opportunity to inspect it prior to its purchase. In its abandonment, the house had deteriorated and when they moved in, it was not the grand house that their memories portrayed. Living in Philadelphia following the war, then Washington as Vice President for eight years and President for 4 years, John never really lived there until 1801. During his absence, Abigail renovated and added onto the house to make it more suitable for entertaining heads of state such as Monroe and Lafayette. When John retired in 1801, he returned to Peace field to work on his papers and create a library of several thousand books (now in the Boston Public Library).

Abigail died in 1818 and John in 1826, and subsequent to that, Peace field was home for his son John Quincy Adams (sixth president of the United States) and then Charles Francis Adams (ambassador to England and son of John Quincy Adams). Charles Francis married a rich woman allowing them to modernize the house as well as to enlarge it. After John Quincy's death, Charles Francis built a stone library (a protection against fire) to house 12,000 volumes of the Adams' family library.

The garden is bordered by the house on the east, the library on the north and a park on the west. A formal garden with boxwood borders and straight gravel paths, it is about 50 yards long, and it mimics the

Tuileries that Abigail might have enjoyed while in Paris, although on a much smaller scale. There is no specific tour of the garden, but the tours of the two farm houses and Peace field with its stone library are excellent and last about two hours. A movie preceding the tour reviews the contributions that the four generations of the Adams family have made and the relationship that each generation of Adams has had to Peace field.

Peace field from the garden

ELEANOR CABOT BRADLEY RESERVATION

2468B Washington Street (Route 138), Canton, MA 02021
Website: www.thetrustees.org
Phone: 781-821-2996
Season: Year round daily
Hours and Days of Operation: Daily sunrise to sunset; There are no regular
     house tours. Maps of the property are available in the parking lot.
Entry Fees: Free

The Cabot Bradley Reservation in Canton, Massachusetts is a 90-acre estate consisting of a farm, open fields, woodlands with three miles of hiking trails, formal gardens and a Georgian Style house. It is uniquely located between the interchange of of Routes 95 and 93, two of the busiest highways outside of nearby Boston. For the weary traveler, it is an island of rural tranquility.

The property lies south of the great Blue Hill, and in the 1650's, was part of a 6,000 acre Indian plantation created for the Indians displaced by the colonization of Boston. By the early 1700's, most of the plantation had been sold since the tribe had either been killed or had migrated further west. In the early 1800's, the region became a popular location for Bostonians to hike the Blue Hills and fish. Taverns were built to service this "Blue-Blooded" group. One of these taverns was Cleary Tavern, and in 1865, Samuel Cabot purchased and converted the tavern into a weekend and summer retreat because the advent of train service made the area easily accessible to Boston. Cabot was a physician, abolitionist and a leader of women's suffrage. Samuel did little to the tavern and property except to remove the barn. When he died in 1885, he left the property to his son, Arthur Tracy Cabot (1852-1912). Also a physician, Arthur had greater aspirations for the property since, at that time, large country estates were being built in the area. He purchased more acreage, moved the old tavern off the property, and in 1902 hired Charles Platt to design a Georgian-style house as well as gardens and the grounds. The house and gardens were designed to interact with each component equal in importance and giving balance to the other. The Italianate garden and its allée to the south, the house, and the entering drive sit on one axis. When designed, the allée allowed for views of Neponset Valley to the south and Blue Hill to the north. Unfortunately, these views are now partially obstructed by the growth of trees. There was also enough farming to allow self-sufficiency.

Arthur died in 1912 and his wife in 1944, at which time the estate was acquired by Arthur's niece, Eleanor Cabot Bradley and her husband, Ralph Bradley. Both Bradleys were interested in farming, horticulture and landscape design. Eleanor had attended the Cambridge School of Architecture and Landscape Architecture and later took horticultural courses. Ralph, an executive at the Cabot Corporation, was interested in farming, and together they renovated and modernized the house, enhanced the farming activity of the property, and added a pond for fishing. Eleanor also created a vegetable garden, a camellia pit, and transformed a dell on the property into a Japanese walkway with dogwoods, hollies and an iris pool. After Ralph's death, Mrs. Bradley worked with The Trustees to preserve the house and property and on her death in 1990, The Trustees took possession of the property.

The gardens and the walking trails are open daily, and there are maps in the parking lot to guide visitors. The house is open for touring without a set schedule, so a visit to the website should identify opportunities. The house sits on a hill with the entrance drive to the north and Italian gardens to the south. Beyond the garden is an allée that allows views of the Neponset Valley. To the west of the house are fields with sheep and a llama grazing around the fish pond. To the east are the barns, the camellia pit, and the kitchen gardens that can be reached by a woodland path lined with rhododendrons.

Eleanor Cabot Bradley Reservation - Courtesy of N. Gordon of The Trustees

FREDERICK LAW OLMSTED NATIONAL HISTORIC SITE

99 Warren Street, Brookline, MA 02445
Web site: www.nps.gov/frla
Phone: 617-566-1689
Dates of Open Season: Variable-check website
Hours and Days of Operation: Variable-check website
Entry Fees: Free

In 1883, Frederick Law Olmsted purchased a farmhouse with 2 acres in Brookline, Massachusetts just outside of Boston. He called his small estate "Fairsted". He moved to Boston because he had made a commitment to build a five mile long park that extended from the Charles River to developing suburban neighborhoods within the city. This linear park is known as "The Emerald Necklace", and it was meant to not only act as a buffer to the cruelty of expanding urbanization, but also to address health problems created by the polluted swamps that permeated the "Emerald Necklace".

Olmsted was a largely self-educated Renaissance man. Born in Hartford, Connecticut in 1822 to a relatively affluent family, he had minimal formal education, but was an avid reader and was encouraged by his family to appreciate the natural world. Having difficulty finding a career in early adulthood, Olmsted first served as an apprentice surveyor, and then as a sailor on a ship that went to China for a year. His father then purchased a farm on Staten Island where Frederick practiced scientific farming for four years. On a walking tour of Europe in 1850 at age 28, he discovered Birkenhead Park in England. It was this park that became the inspiration for the work of his life, and he and successors of his design firm would go on to develop similar parks in almost every state of the United States (44 out of 50). It also inspired him to write a book "Walks and Talks - An American Farmer in Europe". This book was well-received and helped him obtain a job as a correspondent at the New York Times. His literary career brought him into contact with many influential New Yorkers, and partly due to these contacts, he obtained the appointment of Superintendent of the Central Park Commission that was charged with designing and constructing Central Park. Calvert Vaux, an English architect and landscape designer, collaborated with Olmsted, and it was this relationship that fostered Olmsted's career in landscape architecture. Because of the success of Central Park and then Prospect Park, also in New York City, the leaders of American cities recognized the value of parks as a check on the urbanization triggered by the Industrial Revolution, and as a result, they commissioned Calvert and Olmsted to build parks for their own cities. Their partnership lasted until 1872, at which time Olmsted established his own firm and eventually brought in his two sons, John (1852-1920) and Frederick Jr. (1870-1952), both of whom had apprenticed with their father.

In 1895, Frederick retired and the firm was renamed Olmsted Brothers. The firm continued on until Frederick Jr. retired in 1950. During the life of the firm, it was involved in over 6,000 projects that among others, included the U.S. Capitol grounds, Stanford University and the city park systems of dozens of cities as well as Acadia National Park.

Frederick Sr. was a man of many talents who strongly believed in the democratic ideal of allowing access to nature for all men through parks. He wrote a report, as part of a delegation to study the disposition of Yosemite Valley, that supported the role of government in protecting places of natural beauty, so that they would be available to the public in perpetuity. This report was responsible for making Yosemite Valley a park, which initially was turned over to the state of California and eventually to the federal government. The philosophy underlying the report was also critical in establishing a justification for creating a National Park Service in 1916 under Woodrow Wilson.

Fairsted was Frederick's home until his death in 1903. It was also his place of business, which grew to about 70 employees. To accomplish this dual function, the farmhouse was added on to several times. In 1980, the National Park Service acquired Fairsted and all its records. The records include correspondence, bills, but more importantly, 66,000 photographs and 139,000 drawings and plans for projects. The protection of these documents was initiated, because it was felt that these documents were critical in the maintenance and restoration of thousands of public places across the United States.

The tour of Fairsted focuses more on the business side of Fairsted than the domestic side, although this is also touched upon. The gardens are an Olmsted park in miniature. One enters through a very rustic arched gateway constructed of spruce poles and covered with euonymus vines. A circular drive leads to the house whose view is obscured by a hillock centered by a hemlock covered with vines. To the right is a stone path leading down from the driveway to a naturalistic hollow planted with bulbs and ground cover. On the left of the driveway is a small woodland path that passes through a rock garden between rhododendrons and leads to an open lawn. Surrounding the lawn are densely planted trees that line a stonewall and then ascend the hill behind. The view over this lawn to the trees from the house imparts the sense of a protected wilderness.

Olmsted House

◼ ISABELLA STEWART GARDNER MUSEUM

25 Evans Way, Boston, MA 02155
Website; www.gardnermuseum.org
Phone: 617-566-1401
Season: Year round
Hours and Days of Operation: 11 AM to 5 PM everyday day except Thursday
    when it is 11 AM to 9 PM. Tuesdays the Museum is CLOSED.
Tours: Check website or call
Entry Fees: $15 Adults/ $12 Seniors/ $5 College Students

Isabella Stewart Gardner was born on April 14, 1840 to David and Adelia Stewart in New York City, of all places, as she was to become a legend in Boston. Her father, a second-generation Scotsman and according to Isabella, a descendent of King Fergus and Mary Queen of Scots, was a well to do businessman who was comfortable but not rich like the Vanderbilts. As a child, Isabella (Belle) is described as a "handful" who enjoyed the antics of her male peers because of their more mischievous ways. She was reported to be very headstrong and had to be farmed out to her paternal grandmother to relieve the rest of the family. Her passions were dance, gymnastics and languages as well as painting with watercolors. At age 16, she was sent to a French finishing school where she befriended Julia Gardner, the sister of her future husband, John L. Jr. or just plain "Jack". The Gardners were an important Boston family with great wealth derived from sailing ships and eventually railroads. Jack was considered a prize by the Boston debutantes, but Isabella won out with her wit, dancing and sense of adventure and they were married in 1860.

The early years of her marriage were difficult for Isabella because she desperately wanted children, but was having difficulty at a time when her three sister-in -laws were having their 2nd or 3rd children. In addition, she was being given a subtle snub by her female contemporaries in Boston who were jealous of her marriage and her spontaneity. Happiness arrived on June 18, 1863 when John Lowell Gardner II was born, but was followed by tragedy when in March of 1865, he died of complications of pneumonia. That same summer Isabella became pregnant again but lost the child during her pregnancy, and was told that she would not be able to have children again. Following this, she developed an undiagnosable illness (probably depression), and a trip to Europe was recommended. On this trip she developed a greater taste for music and fashion, becoming a devotee of the fashion designer, Charles Frederick Worth of Paris. She brought back to Boston these new fashions that were initially met with raised eyebrows, but eventually accepted by the grand dames of Boston. Her illness was cured by her trip.

In June 1875, Jack Gardner's brother, Joseph, died leaving three sons to the guardianship of Isabella and Jack. Taking this guardianship seriously and concerned about their education, Isabella started a period of self education by attending lectures at Harvard with Charles Eliot Norton amongst others. Professor Norton suggested to Isabella that she collect things other than gowns and jewels. This marked the beginning of years of collecting. She found that she enjoyed intellectual stimulation and began to invite young artists whether they be musicians, writers or painters, to her "boudoir" at her house at 152 Beacon Street. One of these young artists was Bernard Berenson, the son of Lithuanian immigrants, who while at Harvard met Mrs. G and when denied a Harvard scholarship to Europe, was sponsored by Isabella and other wealthy Bostonians. It was Berenson and her friendships with James Whistler and John Singer Sargent that in 1892 inspired the Gardners to begin collecting art. By the late 1890's their collection of art had outgrown the space at their Beacon Street house. When Jack unexpectedly died in 1898, Isabella hired Willard Sears to design a Venetian Palace to be her new home as well as a museum for her collections. The choice of the Venetian palace reflected her love of Venice where over many summers, she had rented the Plaza Barboza from friends. She purchased land in the Fenway, a newly developed part of Boston that was part of Olmsted's newly created park called the "Emerald Necklace". From 1898 to 1901, she was totally involved with the construction and planning of her masterpiece. It was a period of great stress to her architect, but of great creativity for Isabella, as she was involved with every detail of the creation of her museum from choosing paint textures, to the placement of windows and doors and, of course, the organization of her collections. The crown jewel of the palace was the inner courtyard covered by a glass roof. Bella had always been a great horticulturist, and she designed the courtyard to bring light into the interior of the house as well as to serve as a garden.

In November 1901, the servants and she moved into the yet to be completed palace, as 152 Beacon St. had been stripped of its furnishings, doors and architectural details. On January 1, 1903, Isabella opened her Venetian Palace to friends for the first time with 50 members of The Boston Symphony Orchestra playing as entertainment. All agreed that the palace was an "architectural masterpiece". Although she would continue to live there with all her servants, she maintained that the house was a museum, although it was only open two weeks in September and April, and only 200 visitors were allowed on those days. In 1919 Isabella had a stroke resulting in weakness on her right side. For a long time she admitted only to having the flu and refused to publicly acknowledge her real condition. Because of her paralysis, she had herself carried around in a gondola chair and only admitted to having a bad knee. Despite her disability, she continued to be very active until her death in 1924.

The museum is open year round every day except Tuesdays. One enters the museum through the new wing, designed by Renzo Piano and completed in 2012. While still alive, Isabella spent hours codifying Instructions as to how her museum should be run, and on her death her will was very specific that the structure of her house-museum and her collections not be changed. If the terms of her will were to be violated, then her Venetian Palace and collections were to be given to Harvard College. The new wing, which provides more space for a green house, classrooms and concert hall, etc., does not violate Isabella's wishes, since it is not attached to the museum except by a glass corridor which leads the visitor Into a hallway and into the four story glass covered courtyard. This courtyard garden was created with gravel paths, benches, and statuary as well as cloisters. Tall tropical trees and plants, hanging blooming vines and flowering plants, changed nine times a year, make this flowering paradise a magnet for one's visit since most of the rooms of this Venetian Palace look onto this space. Tours of the palace may be either self-guided or guided.The guided tours of the palace focus on Isabella's life, and specific paintings and treasures collected by the Gardners on their abundant travels abroad. After the guided tour, visitors may wander around the rooms of the palace and enjoy this magnificent house and its collections. Finally, there is an outdoor garden designed by Michael Van Valkenburgh and created in 2013. It is a woodland area located outside of the palace and planted with 60 trees, ground cover, flowering seasonal bulbs and perennials, and intersected with a meandering pathway that neither seems to begin or end.

■ LONGFELLOW HOUSE-WASHINGTON'S HEADQUARTERS NATIONAL HISTORIC SITE

105 Brattle Street, Cambridge, MA 02138
Website: www.nps.gov/long
Phone: 617-876-4491
Season: End of May to end of October
Hours and Days of Operation: Wednesday through Sunday, 9:30-5:00 PM
House Tours: Wednesday through Sunday, 9:30- 5:00 PM
Entry Fees: Free

Located in Cambridge, Massachusetts, Longfellow House is most famous as the home of George Washington and Henry Wadsworth Longfellow. The original Georgian house and farm were built by Major John Vassall in 1759. Vassall was loyal to the British, and as the political climate heated up prior to the Declaration of Independence, he fled to England. In June of 1775, one month after the Battle of Bunker Hill, George Washington was appointed Commander of the Continental Army, and in July moved to Cambridge to take charge of his command. He and his wife moved into Longfellow House. While in Cambridge, Washington reorganized and trained the army while keeping an eye on the British Army located across the Charles River in Boston. In what was to become Longfellow's study, he met with Revolutionary leaders such as John Adams, Benedict Arnold and Benjamin Franklin.

In 1791, Andrew Craigie, the nation's first Apothecary General and a land speculator, purchased the house and property. He enlarged the house to such a degree that it became known as "Castle Craigie". In 1819,

Mr. Craigie died, leaving the house, 135 acres of gardens and orchards and significant debts. Consequently, Mrs. Craigie needed to sell off much of the land and to take on boarders, one of whom was a young Harvard professor named Henry Wadsworth Longfellow. At age 36, Longfellow, the son of a prominent lawyer from Portland, Maine, married Fanny Appleton in 1843. His father-in-law, a very wealthy textile manufacturer, bought the house for them, and Henry and Fanny raised five children there. Henry taught language (he knew eight languages) and literature at Harvard until 1854 when he retired to write poetry. This he did very successfully, and his works were well received in the United States as well as in Europe. Some of his most famous epic poems are "Evangeline", "The Song of Hiawatha", and "Paul Revere's Ride". Henry and Fanny were very proud of Washington's relationship to their house and allowed visitors to view the rooms from which Washington first led the war. Because of his writings, Longfellow was a magnet for leaders of the literary world such as Emerson, Hawthorne, Julia Ward Howe and Dickens as well as leaders of the political world (Charles Sumner, a leading abolitionist of his time). The house was a meeting place for these important figures of American history.

In 1861, Fanny died after her dress caught fire, and after Longfellow died in 1882, his daughter, Alice, lived on the upper floors and opened the bottom floor as a museum in 1913. She died in 1928, but her nephew Henry Wadsworth Longfellow Dana, continued to live there until 1950. Both Henry and Alice were committed to perpetuating Henry Sr.'s legacy by maintaining and organizing his papers, books and paintings, as well as the furnishings of the house. In 1972, the National Park Service took control of the house and gardens and has since operated it as a museum.

Hourly tours of the house take place from the end of May to the end of October, The schedule for garden tours is variable depending on staffing. Henry and Fanny's collection of art, which included landscapes, portraits and sculptures, is intact. The family's library of over 12,000 volumes is preserved, and the furnishings are original to the house. The grounds of Longfellow House include two acres on one side of Brattle Street. On the other side of Brattle Street lies Longfellow Park (owned by the city of Cambridge, but once owned by Longfellow) that allows for extended views of the Charles River. To the rear and side of the house is a large enclosed garden that is a Colonial Revival-style garden with a pergola and boxwood parterres. The garden underwent a renovation in 1904, and in 1925, it was redesigned by Ellen Biddle Shipman. The gardens continue to be well-maintained by the park service as well as local volunteers.

Longfellow House-Courtesy of the National Park Service
Longfellow House - Washington's Headquarters National Historic Site

■ CODMAN ESTATE

34 Codman Road, Lincoln, MA 01773
Website: historicnewengland.org and enter zip code
Phone: 617-994-6690
Season: June 1-October 15th
Days and Hours of Operation: HOUSE TOURS LIMITED: 2nd and 4th
Saturdays of the month 10 AM- 2 PM. Grounds may be toured from
dawn to dusk.
Tour Fees: Adult $10/ Seniors $9/ Students $5

The Codman Estate, otherwise known as the Grange, dates back to
1741 when Chambers Russell built a Georgian mansion on a large tract of
land in Lincoln, Massachusetts. He ran it as a farm and eventually passed
it on to his great nephew, Charles Russell Codman, in 1790. Because
Charles was a minor, his father, John Codman, took control and upgraded
the property. He increased the acreage to about 650 acres, doubled the
size of the house, and remodeled it in the style of a Federal style mansion.
Finally, he softened the landscape by rounding out pathways and by
adding more trees to screen the farm buildings. His intent was to create a
more natural landscape, a fashion that was very popular in England at that
time. John was influenced by English landscape architecture because, as a
wealthy shipping merchant, he traveled a great deal. After John's death in
1803, his son, Charles Russell Codman, came of age and took possession
of the estate. Charles had no interest in the estate. He was a collector who
liked to travel, and in order to support his lifestyle, he gradually sold the
entire estate.

For 55 years the Codmans no longer owned the property - a fact that the next generation regretted. Charles's son Ogden and his wife Sarah repurchased the estate in 1861 to use as a country weekend house. The house was again renovated, enlarged and modernized. Ogden became very interested in agriculture and applied modern techniques to improving the farm. The Codmans also owned a lot of real estate in Boston, and as a result of the Boston Great Fire in 1872, the finances of the family were seriously compromised. Because of this Ogden, Sarah and their 5 children were forced to move to Europe where living was less expensive. They lived in France for several years while renting out the farm and house for additional income. As their finances stabilized, they moved back to the Grange full time, no longer keeping a house in Boston.

On their return to Lincoln, Sarah and the eldest son, Ogden Jr. took on the job of running the estate as his father seems to have become less interested in both the estate and perhaps his family. Ogden Jr. became a well respected architect designing houses in Newport and New York City (see Kykuit and the Mount). He worked with his mother to redecorate and modernize the house. Ogden Jr. was the only child to earn a living and marry, but he never had children as his wife died early on. The other four children continued to live at the Grange. Sarah died in 1922 and the youngest child, Dorothy, died in 1968. As early as the 1920's, Ogden Jr. made arrangements, so that at the death of the last child, the house and gardens would be given to Historic New England for their long term protection.

During their lifetime, both Sarah and Dorothy worked hard to maintain the two gardens. The Italian garden, which lies to the northwest of the house, is a sunken walled garden with a central pool. A pergola stands at one end, and at the other end are sculptures and fountains. Sarah and Ogden Jr. designed the Italian Garden around 1900, and it became a labor of love for Sarah until her death. The other garden next to the Carriage House was created by Dorothy and was designed as an English Cottage garden. Both gardens are well-maintained.

A visit to the Grange is certainly worthwhile. Unfortunately, access to the house is quite limited, since it is only open for tours Saturday mornings every other week. The tours are interesting because the house still contains the original furnishings, books and art collection of the family. The art collection contains one portrait by Gilbert Stuart and two portraits by John Copley. Reflecting the English landscape style, the grounds are beautiful, and the property is surrounded by open meadows, woods, trails and farmland.

Codman Garden - Courtesy of Historic New England

NEW ENGLAND WILD FLOWER SOCIETY'S GARDEN IN THE WOODS

184 Hemenway Road, Framingham, MA 01701
Website: www.newenglandwild.org
Phone: 508-877-7630
Season: Mid April-October 15th
Hours and Days of Operation: Daily 10 AM- 5 PM
Garden Tours: See website or call to schedule

Garden in the Woods is located 21 miles west of Boston and comprises 45 acres with more than 2 miles of pathways through the woods, around a pond and a bog and over a stream. The glacial terrain has created a varied landscape of ridges and valleys. It is now the headquarters of the New England Wild Flower Society whose mission is to conserve and promote the region's native plants to ensure healthy, biologically diverse landscapes.

Garden in the Woods was conceived by Will Curtis, a Cornell-trained, landscape architect. In 1931, he purchased 30 acres of a gravel pit from the Old Colony Railroad for $1,000. His intent was to create a site to grow North American wildflowers with a focus on New England wildflowers. He and his partner, Dick Stiles, wanted to observe the conditions that either enabled wildflowers to flourish or to do poorly. By 1953, they had a collection of over 2,000 species planted among the various pathways and woodlands of their property. They continued their work until the early 1960's when they realized they needed help to combat the threats of local development. For this reason, they gave the garden to the Wild Flower Society.

The walk starts at the Visitor Center where maps of the garden are available as well as books which focus on native plants and horticulture. Plants and trees can also be purchased at the center. Garden in the Woods is comprised of meandering pathways through naturalistic garden displays as well as habitat-based displays, showcasing the rich diversity of the native plants of New England. The Gardens support over 1500 species, most of which are native to the eco-regions of New England. Many of the plants in the collection are labeled, but more signage would be helpful.

Leading off the cultivated trails are hiking trails that follow along ridgelines, hollows and a stream. Garden in the Woods has also set aside a nature area where younger children may play. Finally, there are areas of the garden committed to experimentation and education that travelers may find helpful for their own gardens.

STEVENS-COOLIDGE PLACE

137 Andover Street, North Andover MA. 01845
Website: www.thetrustees.org
Phone: 978-682-3580
Season: Year round
Days and Hours of Operation: Garden and Grounds open dawn to dusk
House Tours: No regularly scheduled tours
Entry Fees: Free

Located in North Andover, Massachusetts, Ashdale Farm (Stevens-Coolidge Place) dates back to 1729 when the Stevens family acquired the farm and built a Federal-style farmhouse. Several generations of Stevens continued to occupy the farm until 1914 when John Gardner Coolidge and his wife Helen Stevens (a descendant of the original owner) inherited the property. They intended to use the farm as a country retreat to escape the heat of Boston and as a place to experiment with horticultural ideas acquired during numerous travels around the world.

John Gardner (1863-1936) was the nephew of Isabella Stewart Gardner and the great-great-grandson of Thomas Jefferson. After graduating from Harvard in 1884, he briefly worked for Frederick Law Olmsted and then traveled to the Far East and Europe for several years. An avid photographer, in 1898, he photographed the Spanish-American War, including the sinking of the USS Maine. Apparently, his travel experiences both to Cuba and later the Philippines, allowed him to enter the diplomatic service with postings in Pretoria, South Africa during the Boer War, Peking, China after the Boxer Rebellion, Mexico and Nicaragua.

In 1904, at the age of 41, he married Helen Stevens who had previously served as a companion to his mother. They took possession of the Stevens farm in 1914 and began a several-year process of transforming the property from a working farm to a country estate. To help them with this effort, they hired Joseph Chandler in 1918 to redesign the main house. The architectural style of the remodeled house was a Neo- Georgian Colonial Revival, a style of architecture that Chandler had written about and incorporated into many of his houses including the renovation of Paul Revere's house. The outcome of the redesign was a much bigger house that opened up to and incorporated the gardens and fields beyond.

John and Helen filled the house with objects acquired on their many travels all over the world which includes John's collection of Chinese porcelains and European decorative arts. The house also contains a significant collection of American antiques. John died in 1936, and Helen in 1962. Since they had no children, they left the house with its original contents and property with 91 acres to The Trustees to be protected in perpetuity.

Both John and Helen were interested in gardening, and working again with Joseph Chandler, they added several gardens to an existing garden created by Helen's sister in 1907. Sitting directly behind the house, Helen's garden (designed by Louisa Bancroft Stevens) can be viewed from an elevated brick terrace and French doors in the parlor. On one side of this garden is a sunken Italianate rose garden and a greenhouse. On the other side is cutting garden and a wildflower garden behind the kitchen. As you stand in each of these gardens, your eye leads you out onto open pastures and an orchard. Finally, there is a an elaborate French potager garden created in the early 1930's for Helen, who wished to reproduce the chateau gardens that she and John had seen in France during World War I. This garden is separate from the house, but abuts a serpentine wall. It is divided into quadrants planted with a mixture of perennials, annuals and vegetables and defined by gravel pathways. The gardens are open from dawn to dusk, and guided tours of the house are primarily scheduled on the weekends. The house tours are well worth scheduling, as the contents of the house are original and include art and treasures collected on the Coolidges' travels around the world.

Stevens-Coolidge Place

THE NORTH SHORE
OF BOSTON

Four of the ten houses (Castle Hill, Long Hill, Hammond Castle, and Beauport) were built during the "Gilded Age" or the early 20th century to provide an escape for their owners from the heat and congestion of the city. For the most part, the houses were summer and weekend retreats, except in the case of Hammond Castle, where its owner maintained his principal residence as well as his research laboratories. The North Shore, at that time, offered the ocean and a rolling countryside with cooling summer breezes. The rest of the sites were built around the time of the American Revolutionary War at a time when the rivers and harbors from Salem to Portsmouth created great wealth through maritime trade (Glen Magna Farms, Moffatt- Ladd House, Langdon House and Hamilton House). The oldest house, the John Whipple House, was built in the 1640's with profits from commerce on the Ipswich River. The houses of the Revolutionary era are less opulent with smaller grounds and gardens than those from the "Gilded Age", but well worth visiting given the superior level of architectural detail and workmanship. Fuller Garden is the only garden on the north Shore which stands alone without a house.

INFORMATION REGARDING DAYS AND HOURS OF OPERATION AS WELL AS FEES AT EACH SITE ARE SUBJECT TO CHANGE AND IT IS BEST TO PHONE OR CHECK THE WEBSITE FOR EACH LOCATION FOR UP-TO- DATE INFORMATION.

North Shore of Boston

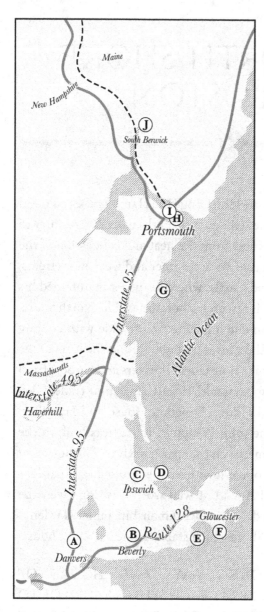

(A) Glen Magna Farms
29 Ingersoll St, Danvers, MA

(B) Long Hill
572 Essex St, Beverly, MA

(C) Whipple House
54 S Main St, Ipswich, MA

(D) Crane Estate
290 Argilla Rd, Ipswich, MA

(E) Hammond Castle
88 Hesperus Ave, Gloucester, MA

(F) Beauport
the Sleeper-McCann House
*75 Eastern Point Blvd,
Gloucester, MA*

(G) Fuller Gardens
*10 Willow Ave,
North Hampton, NH*

(H) Langdon House
143 Pleasant St, Portsmouth, NH

(I) Moffatt-Ladd House
154 Market St, Portsmouth, NH

(J) Hamilton House
*40 Vaughans Ln,
South Berwick, ME*

GLEN MAGNA FARMS

29 Ingersoll Street, Danvers, MA 01923
Website: www.glenmagnafarms.org
Phone: 978-774-9165
Season: Early May to mid October
Days and Hours of Operation: Garden is open Monday through Friday 9 AM
    to dusk and on Saturdays+Sundays 9 AM until noon.
Tours: House tours are by reservation only (call 978-774-9165) and include a
    box lunch on Wednesdays at 11 AM May through October
Entry Fees: $2 contribution for garden entry and house tour is $20

Danvers, Massachusetts is a typical suburb of Boston with miles of shopping malls and developments, but it is also the home of Glen Magna Farms, originally the summer estate which Joseph Peabody acquired in 1812.

Joseph (1757-1844) was born in Middleton, Massachusetts and was the ninth of 12 children. At age eight, he was sent to live with his sister to help with the farm and he later became an itinerant cobbler. In his late teens and during the Revolutionary War, he went to sea on a privateer with established merchants- the Derbys and the Cabots. He was able to rise from seaman, to captain, to part owner. By 1810, he owned a large fleet of merchant ships that participated in both the "China" trade and "Pepper" trade with Sumatra. By 1812, he was the wealthiest man in Salem.

Understanding the need for a formal education, Joseph spent a year studying reading, writing and the art of polite conversation with Reverend Elias Smith. This interlude provided him with not only an education, but a wife. In 1791, he married Smith's daughter, Catherine, who unfortunately died of tuberculosis in 1793. He then married the Reverend's other daughter, Elizabeth, and together they had four children. During the War of 1812, Joseph purchased 20 acres of land in the town of Danvers as a summer retreat and as a refuge from a possible invasion of Salem in the War of 1812. Over the ensuing years, he purchased more land, expanding the farm to 330 acres. In 1815, the garden to the south of the house was added under the guidance of George Heussler, a noted Alsatian gardener. Joseph died in 1844, and the estate was eventually inherited by his granddaughter, Ellen Peabody Endicott.

Ellen and her husband, the Secretary of War under Grover Cleveland, continued to use the estate as a summer retreat, and in the 1890's engaged Little, Brown and Moore to upgrade and restore the mansion to the Colonial Revival style. Under the guidance of the Olmsted brothers, the approach and layout of the estate was reconfigured at the same time. The design of the original garden was maintained, but an Italianate and a shrubbery garden were added in 1890 under the supervision of Joseph Chamberlain, son-in-law of Ellen Peabody Endicott and father of Neville Chamberlain (Prime Minister of England prior to WW II). Finally, an enclosed rose garden with a colonial tower at one end was added in the 1900's. When William Crowninshield Endicott died in 1936, he was the last descendant of Joseph Peabody to live at Glen Magna Farms. In 1963, the Danvers Historical Society purchased the house and 11 acres of the grounds and gardens. An additional 120 acres of the farm was purchased by the town to be used as a park and walking trails.

The mansion is open to the public on a limited basis with pre-arranged tours. The gardens are open dawn to dusk except on Saturdays and Sundays, when they are open 9:00am - 12:00pm. The three gardens are well-maintained although unmarked. The estate itself is surrounded by farmland and open fields which are separated from the gardens by gates and pathways meandering through the rhododendrons. The original driveway is an allée that borders the formal gardens and ends in a circular drive shaded by towering trees dating back to 1812.

The rear of Glen Magna from the garden

▪ LONG HILL

572 Essex Street, Beverly, MA 01915
Website: www.thetrustees.org
Season: Year round
Hours and Days of Operation: Year round: 8 AM- 5 PM with peak bloom in
    May and June
House Tours: None: Maps of the Garden available in the parking lot
Entry Fees: Free

Unlike most well-heeled Bostonians who built large summer
estates in the early 1900's on the coast of the North Shore of Boston to
take advantage of the cool ocean breezes, Ellery and Mabel Sedgwick
purchased a 114-acre farm in inland Beverly, Massachusetts. The
Sedgwicks wanted to have land to extend their horticultural interests.
Mabel was an accomplished gardener and author of a popular book, "The
Garden, Month by Month".

Ellery Sedgwick, a graduate of Groton and Harvard, was a descendant
of a long line of a Stockbridge, Massachusetts family with literary
interests. After teaching classics at Groton for a year, Ellery also pursued
a literary career by working at a series of magazines (Leslie's Monthly,
American Magazine, and McClure's) until 1908 when he purchased The
Atlantic Monthly. Founded in 1854 as a literary magazine by Emerson,
Longfellow, Holmes and Harriet Beecher Stowe, it was struggling with a
circulation of 15,000 and a deficit of $5,000 a year. By discovering new
writers such as Hemingway, Ellery made the magazine successful and
sold the magazine in 1938 with a readership of 137,000.

In 1916, the Sedgwicks purchased the farm and moved into the farmhouse. At about the same time, Ellery discovered a house that was to be torn down in Charleston, South Carolina. Not only did the Federalist style architecture become the inspiration for a new house at Long Hill, but the paneling, doors, mantle pieces and exterior trim were shipped to Beverly to be incorporated into the new house. After living in the farmhouse at the bottom of the hill for nine years, they moved into the new house at the top of the hill in 1925. Having already developed orchards and defined the operations of the farm, Mabel designed and implemented a series of gardens around the house. The gardens were a series of rooms centered on the house porches and terraces, and bordered by hedges and gates that lead down pathways to woodland walkways. Many of the these garden rooms took advantage of the height of the property because windows created by allées through the woods allowed views of the surrounding countryside. In 1937, Mabel died and in 1939, Ellery married Marjorie Russell, also an accomplished horticulturist. Marjorie extended the gardens and worked with the Arnold Arboretum to incorporate more species of plants, shrubs and trees (now more than 400) as well as sculptural elements. Ellery and Marjorie lived in the house full-time from 1940 until his death in 1960 and her death in 1979. In 1980, the estate was given to The Trustees. The gardens are now open to the public on a daily basis, and the house is open on a limited basis by reservation only.

Under the Trustees' stewardship, the estate continues to flourish. Inside the first gate of the property is an active farm. As you drive up the hill, you will see the farmhouse where the Sedgwicks first lived. Ascending the hill, one passes through an allée of crabapple trees abutting the orchard that Mabel planted, and eventually, one reaches the circular drive in front of the house centered by an enormous copper beech. The gardens are well-maintained, and the garden's brochure and map is well-written and very helpful. The trees are marked which is important given the variety of species. Many of the sculptural elements of the garden are also explained in the brochure. The vistas from the garden are still present, but the views in summer are more limited due to the foliage. If you are a hiker, there are clearly marked trails that extend from the gardens through the woodlands and up and down the drumlin. The trails are said to be about a mile long.

Long Hill-Courtesy of R. Cheek and The Trustees

■ JOHN WHIPPLE HOUSE

54 South Main Street, Ipswich, MA 01938
Website: www.ipswichmuseum.org
Phone: 978-356-2811
Season: End of May to early October
Hours and Days of Operation: Thursday through Saturday 10 AM-4 PM and
    Sunday 1PM-4 PM
Entry Fees: $10 Adult/ $5 Students 13-17/ Free under 13

Built around 1634, Whipple House is located in Ipswich, Massachusetts on the road to Castle Hill. When John Whipple (1596-1669) bought the house and 6 acres of land in the 1640's, he was a struggling farmer. His son, Captain John Whipple (1625-1683), inherited the house, doubled its size and his family occupied the house over a span of 150 years. Eventually, it became a boarding house and suffered great neglect. When the the house was at risk for demolition in the early 1900's, a group of local citizens stepped in to save it, given its historical significance. In the 1920's, the house was moved to its current location across from the Ipswich Museum on land donated by Mr. Crane of Castle Hill. Although it was moved in the 1920's, the house was not restored until the 1950's. The restoration involved the transformation of its Georgian architecture back to its original Post-Medieval Style by restoring the gables and windows to the house.

The house is available for viewing, and tickets may be purchased through the Ipswich Museum across the street. The house restoration is well done, and the furnishings and paintings, although not original to the house, are consistent with the period. The uses of household implements of the Colonial period are explained and demonstrated. One example is the mechanism which Ipswich housewives used for sewing lace, a product for which Ipswich was quite famous for. The gardens were designed by Arthur Shurcliff in the 1920's to resemble a Colonial garden, but only part of the design was implemented. Immediately outside the front of the house is an enclosed garden with a picket fence. Referred to as a "housewife's garden", it provided seasoning and medicinal herbs for the household. The garden is geometric with raised beds of flowers and herbs separated by gravel paths. A small rose garden is planted in front of the house closer to the road. Behind the house, visitors may view the marsh with a path leading down to the Ipswich River.

Whipple House

CASTLE HILL ON THE CRANE ESTATE

290 Argilla Road, Ipswich, MA 01938
Website: www.thetrustees.org
Phone: 978-356-4351
Season: Daily year round
Hours and Days of Operation: Grounds are open daily 8 AM to sunset. Access
    to the House is variable as are tours so review of Website is preferred.
Tours of the House: check Website
Entry Fees: $10 per car for entry onto the grounds. House fees are variable
    depending on the tours-check Website

A visit to the Crane Estate in Ipswich, Massachusetts, a seaside town
north of Boston, provides the visitor with an opportunity to experience
a house, gardens, 165 acres of surrounding grounds, an additional 1931
acres of woodlands and marshes and one of the premier beaches in
Massachusetts. The house is named "Castle Hill" because it sits on a hill
that looks over the fields, marshes and beaches that can be seen from this
grand house.

In 1637, the town of Ipswich gave the land now occupied by the
Crane estate to John Winthrop Jr., the son of the first Governor of
Massachusetts, so that it could be farmed. It remained a working farm
until the late 1800's when it was transformed into a country estate by the
Brown family. The farmhouse was enlarged and gentrified, and roads and
fields were created to enhance the views.

In 1909, Richard T. Crane Jr. bought the estate from the Brown
family and proceeded to further develop a summer estate. Located two-
thirds of the way up Castle Hill, the rambling farmhouse used by the

Browns was upgraded so that Mrs. Crane's family, the Higginbothams (a wealthy and important family from Chicago), would have a place to stay. Crane engaged the services of Shepley, Rutan, and Coolidge of Boston to build his own family's house on the top of Castle Hill. The house, barns, outbuildings and gardens were Italianate in design. Unfortunately, his wife Florence, finding it dark and musty, did not like the house. After trying to improve the original house, Mr. Crane had the original house torn down in the mid-1920's and hired a Chicago architect to design an airier, lighter, English-style mansion which was 39,000 square feet and had 59 rooms. Taking advantage of the fact that many of England's "great houses" were being demolished because of difficult financial times after World War I, the paneling and floors were imported and used for the interior of the new house. The new house was completed in 1928, and in 1931, Richard died unexpectedly at age 58.

Richard Crane Jr. was the son of Richard Sr. who built the Crane Plumbing fortune by manufacturing pumps and pipes. Richard Jr. began working for the company in his early years and always believed his early association with the company was the best form of education. Richard Sr. died in 1912, and under Richard Jr.'s leadership, the company expanded its range of products to produce bathroom fixtures. By the time of his death, the Crane Company had 300,000 employees. Richard Crane Jr. was a unique employer of his time, because his employees had both stock options and health insurance. In recognition of his caring, the Crane employees gave the two griffin sculptures created by Paul Mansard on the main terrace. His choice of the Ipswich property was unusual in that men of his class and wealth often chose Newport or Bar Harbor, but Richard appeared to desire an escape from the social pressures of being an industrialist in the "Gilded Age". To satisfy his need for a retreat and to protect his privacy and view, he acquired 2,100 acres of surrounding properties and beaches.

Florence Crane continued to spend her summers at Castle Hill until her death in 1949. Having previously given 1,000 acres to The Trustees in 1945, she bequeathed the house and an additional 350 acres to them at her death. Their two children, Cornelius and Florence, continued to live in the area and along with neighbors, added additional acreage to the Crane Estate so that there are now 2,096 acres of beaches, marshes, woodlands, and gardens.

The house and gardens are open to the public seven days a week. The beaches are also open, as are miles of hiking trails. Although the furnishings of the house were sold at Mrs. Crane's death on her instructions, the house has been re-furnished with a great effort to restore the house to its former glory. The allée designed by Shurcliff which measures one-half mile before it reaches the sea, has recently been restored. The Italian garden, designed by the Olmsted Brothers, has also been recently restored and lies down the hill from the house and overlooks the ruins of the old rose garden (designed by Shurcliff) and the marshes beyond. In addition, the estate includes its full complement of outbuildings, including the barn and the bachelor's quarters, as well as miles of hiking trails that follow the old farm roads down to the marshes and beaches.

View of Castle Hill - Courtesy of The Trustees

HAMMOND CASTLE

88 Hesperus Avenue, Gloucester, MA 01930
Website: www.hammondcastle.org
Phone: 978-283-2080
Season: End of May to early October
Days and Hours of Operation: Tuesday through Sunday 10-4 PM
Fees: Adult $10/ Senior $9/ Children under 12 $8

Across Gloucester Harbor from Beauport, one can see Hammond Castle, which was built from 1926 to 1929 by John Hays Hammond Jr. Born in 1888, John was the son of John Sr. who made his fortune in South Africa mining gold and diamonds, and another fortune drilling for oil and mining gold in the United States and Mexico. John Jr. lived in South Africa initially and then in England where at age 10, he developed a love of castles and antiquities. At age 12, he returned to the U.S. to attend Lawrenceville School and then Yale where he studied engineering. Having met Thomas Edison at age 12 and later Alexander Graham Bell, he became interested in radio waves. He graduated from Yale in 1910 and went to work for the U.S. Patent Office to learn how to turn patents into a successful business. About the same time, he established the Hammond Research Corporation in Gloucester, a company that focused on radio guidance systems. In 1914, his guidance system piloted a 40-foot boat on a 120 mile trip without a helmsman. This achievement caught the attention of the Navy, and his research not only led to 437 patents and 800 inventions, but also made him a very rich man. His inventions include numerous radio-controlled devices including the torpedo, the television, the stereo and the variable pitch propeller.

In 1926, at the age of 38, in anticipation of his upcoming marriage to Irene Fenton, he fulfilled his childhood love of castles by purchasing 8 acres of land from his father on Gloucester Harbor and designing and building Hammond Castle. Charles Collens (architect of the Cloisters in New York) may have been the architect, but John apparently took full credit for its design and implementation. The core of the castle was the "Great Hall" which encompassed 2,800 square feet in area and had a 65-foot ceiling. It contained many of his collections of antiquities, armor and objects of the occult and death. It also contains an experimental 8,200-pipe organ (designed by John) which was said to be one of the finest in the world and a draw for some of the finest organists including Virgil Fox and E. Power Biggs. Although John was an agnostic but raised as an Episcopalian, the Great Hall imparts the feeling of the nave of a great cathedral. Next to the dining room is an enclosed courtyard which is centered by a 8.5-foot deep pool (John liked to dive into it from a second floor balcony) and surrounded by a re-creation of a medieval European village as well as trees and tropical plants. In one corner of the courtyard is a nude bronze statue of John given to his wife by John for an anniversary present. One end of the castle was committed to John's laboratories.

The castle sits on the rocky shores of Gloucester Harbor. The garden and lawn behind the castle have a magnificent view of the ocean. The entryway to the castle sits at the bottom of a steep gorge, planted with rhododendrons and trees, which slopes down to a moat, drawbridge, columns and fountains suggestive of a Roman garden. The house and gardens are open Tuesday through Sunday. A map is available for self-guided tours, but there are also hourly guided tours and a video that details John's life and accomplishments and the history of the house.

John died in 1965 and left the castle to the Catholic church who used the property for a few years until 1975 when it was acquired by Virgil Fox, the organist, for $68,000 (original cost $500,000 in 1926). Unable to afford it, Fox later sold it to a private non-profit foundation which now operates the castle as a museum. Although the church discarded many of the furnishings and artwork, the museum is full of objects original to Hammond's lifetime.

Hammond Castle

BEAUPORT, THE SLEEPER-MCCANN HOUSE

75 Eastern Point Boulevard, Gloucester, MA 01930
Website: www.historicnewengland.org and enter zip code
Phone: 978-283-0800
Season: End of May to Mid October
Hours and Days of Operation: Tuesday-Saturday 10 AM - 4 PM
House Tours: 10 AM- 4 PM
Entry Fees: Adult $15/ Seniors $12/ Students $8

Beauport looks over the outer harbor of Gloucester, Massachusetts and was the creation of Henry Davis Sleeper or just plain "Harry". Born in 1878, he was the third son of a Civil War hero from a prominent Boston family who resided on Beacon Hill in the winter and Marblehead in the summer. Harry was the youngest and a sickly child, and for this reason received most of his education at home. During his youth, he developed an interest in antiques and a proclivity for collecting. His father died in 1891, and in 1902, his mother sold the summer house in Marblehead.

Harry discovered the site of Beauport in 1907 after a visit to a good friend, A. Piatt Andrew, who was a Harvard economist who not only taught FDR, but also served as Assistant Secretary of the Treasury under Taft. Harry found the neighborhood stimulating, as it was made up of intellectuals and artists. In 1900, he built a small house next to Piatt which he and his mother used as a summer and weekend house. Harry hired and collaborated with Halfdan Hanson, a Norwegian with no formal architectural training, to design the first house as well as subsequent additions until Harry's death in 1934. Early on in the construction of the house, Sleeper became a devotee of architectural salvage, incorporating architectural detail from houses to be demolished into newly created rooms at Beauport. Using salvage and his collection of antiques and other paraphernalia, he was able to stage a scene in each of the rooms of Beauport. Rather than change his stage sets, he would just add on to Beauport so that by his death, there were 44 rooms in the house.

Harry may have worked in the family real estate firm, but this was not where his heart was. After his mother's death in 1917, the house and its interior became a national phenomenon due to articles in the national press about its interior. At this point, Sleeper became an interior designer, first for friends and neighbors, and then for the super rich such as Isabella Gardner and Henry Francis Dupont (Winterthur) on the East Coast, and for stars such as Joan Crawford in Hollywood. With all his success came the financial ability to make further additions to Beauport until there was no more land for additions..

In 1934, Sleeper died of leukemia and left the house and a pile of debt to his brother who was forced to sell the house to Helena Woolworth McCann, the 5 and 10 cent store heiress. The McCanns made some minor changes to Beauport, but the tone of the house and collections were not altered. In 1938, Mrs. McCann died and left the house to her children who gave it to Historic New England in 1942. Harry, coincidently, was one of the founders of this organization whose mission is to protect historically significant houses.

The house is regularly open for tours. Although there are 44 rooms, not all of them are shown due to the small size of some rooms. Visits to each room provide a surprise and frequently a glimpse into another time. The gardens are also quite varied and have recently been restored. As you enter the front gate, your eye travels over a small field made up of Pennsylvania Wood Sedge to a formal but oblong garden outside the front door called the "Sundial Garden". Behind and next to the house are walled gardens and terraces which sit on a 20-foot rocky ledge overlooking Gloucester Harbor.

Front garden at Beauport
Courtesy of Historic New England

FULLER GARDENS

10 Willow Avenue, North Hampton, NH 03862
Website: www.fullergardens.org
Phone: 603-964-5414
Season: Early May-Mid October
Hours and Days of Operation: Daily 10-5:30 PM
Guided Tours: None
Entry Fees: $9 Adults/ $8 Seniors/ $6 Students/ $4 Children under 12

Fuller Gardens is located on the ocean in North Hampton, New Hampshire a 20 minute drive south from Portsmouth. The gardens were once part of the summer estate of Alvin Fuller. Although Mr. Fuller's summer home was removed in 1961 according to his wishes, the gardens remain today with spectacular views of the Atlantic Ocean.

Alvin was a successful businessman, athlete, politician, philanthropist and collector of art. Born in 1878 to a Civil War veteran and printer at the Boston Globe Newspaper, Alvin was forced to leave school at an early age after his father died. He went to work for the Boston Rubber Company (now Converse Rubber) working as a manual laborer 12 hours a day and earning $7.50 a week. After his working day, he continued to educate himself by attending business school. At age 18, after starting a bike repair and dealership in his family's barn, he promoted this business by bike racing and winning New England bike racing championships. In 1899, at age 21, he traveled to Europe using money procured by selling his racing trophies and prize money. He returned from Europe with two French automobiles which he then sold for profit. Recognizing the future potential of the auto business, he became a dealer for Packard and then

Cadillac. By 1920, he was the most successful auto dealer in the U.S. His success can be attributed to his vision, business acumen and marketing genius. He was the first dealer to institute the "Washington's birthday sale" and the concept of "buying over time".

The success of his dealerships allowed him to enter the political arena. He was progressive in his thinking and was asked to run on the Progressive Party ticket for Lieutenant Governor of Massachusetts but refused. He supported FDR's political agenda despite having supported Hoover. With a political career as successful as his business career, he served in the Massachusetts legislature from 1914 to 1916, the U.S. House of Representatives from 1916 to 1920, as Lieutenant Governor of Massachusetts from 1921 to 1924, and Governor of Massachusetts from 1925 to 1929. To become governor, he beat the unbeatable James Michael Curley.

In 1910 he married Viola, a neighbor from Medford and an opera singer. They had four children, and around 1920 they built "Runnymede" in North Hampton as a summer home. They hired Arthur Shurcliff in 1927 to create a garden across the street from the main house and next to the carriage house. In the 1930's, the Olmsted Brothers were engaged to redesign the gardens by adding rosebeds and formal, English perennial borders. Apparently the Fullers rarely entered the gardens, but liked to look out their bedroom window and enjoy them. During the Fuller's lifetime, the gardens were always open to the public both for walking and viewing.

A great philanthropist, Mr Fuller gave his art collection (works by Renoir, Rembrandt, Turner and Gainsborough) to the Boston Museum of Fine Arts and the National Gallery of Art. He also founded the Fuller Foundation which among other things supports the ongoing stewardship of Fuller Gardens.

Fuller Gardens features 3 acres of beautiful, well-maintained gardens. Most of the plants and trees are well marked, making any visit an educational experience. Although there are no tours, the gardens are easy to navigate. Visitors enter the gardens through the first rose garden and continue into a second rose garden displaying over 1700 roses of 150 varieties which are all identified. The roses begin their season-long bloom cycle in mid-June and continue through September. At the back of the property is a greenhouse with cacti, succulents and tropical specimens and a carriage house which faces a long gravel drive bordered by a well-manicured yew hedge. Across the gravel drive, visitors can experience the intimacy and tranquility of the Japanese garden and the colorful display of a very large, enclosed English perennial garden.

GOVERNOR JOHN LANGDON HOUSE

143 Pleasant Street, Portsmouth, NH 03801
Website: www.historicnewengland.org and enter the zip code
Phone: 603-436-3205
Season: June 1-October 15
Hours and Days of Operation: 11 AM- 5 PM; Friday-Sunday (last tour at 4 PM)
House Tours: Friday-Sunday: 11 AM-5 PM (last tour at 4 PM)
Entry Fees: $8 Adults/ $7 Seniors/ $4 Students

Langdon House is another example of a Portsmouth, New Hampshire house built with wealth arising from the growth of the shipping industry around the Revolutionary War. Portsmouth is uniquely located on the Piscataqua River which, because of its high flow, was one of the few rivers on the eastern coast that didn't freeze over in the winter. It also drained the woodlands of Maine and therefore, provided significant timber for the King's Navy. The Piscataqua also made the town of Portsmouth a very important fishing port.

John Langdon was born in 1741 into a Portsmouth family of modest means, and by the age of 22, he had become a ship's captain. Eventually, he purchased his own ships and developed a revolutionary fervor when his profits were affected by British restrictions on trade prior to the war. In December of 1774, he helped lead an attack on Fort William and Mary, a British fort that lay at the head of Portsmouth Harbor, and emptied the fort of its ammunition. As a consequence of his role, he became an important Revolutionary War figure, serving as New Hampshire's representative to the Second Continental Congress. During the war, he built the warships Raleigh, Ranger and America. The Ranger was captained by John Paul Jones. Langdon himself became a privateer, allowing him to attack British ships and pocketing the rewards. All of this made him a very wealthy man. He continued to be active politically and served as President of New Hampshire (Governor) in the 1780's and was appointed to the Constitutional Convention. Langdon was also elected the first President of the U.S. Senate and was said to have informed George Washington of his election to the Presidency. Langdon served as Governor of New Hampshire from 1805-1809 and 1810-1812. During this period, he turned down an offer to serve as Secretary of the Navy under Jefferson and to be a candidate as Vice President under Madison.

In 1777, he married Elizabeth Shelburne and had two children, one of whom died in infancy, leaving Eliza. In 1784, he began the construction of his Georgian mansion on a hill on the outskirts of Portsmouth. From this house, he was able to view his shipyard without being exposed to the activities and stench emanating from the wharves. It took several years to complete the house, because the house was large and the Rococo architectural detail was very elaborate. The house was a statement of his wealth and importance in the community. Reputed to have Portsmouth's largest parlor, the house became a center of social activity. George Washington visited the house, but did not stay there.

John Langdon died in 1819, and his daughter, Eliza, who had married well and had her own house, never really moved into the house. From 1836 - 1877, the house was owned by an Episcopal minister and during that time, the southeast corner burned and was restored in the Greek Revival style. In 1877, Woodbury Langdon, a great-great-great-nephew of John Langdon and a successful New York businessman, bought the house for his mother. At his mother's death in 1902, he hired McKim, Mead, and White to modernize the house and to add a wing to the house to accommodate a dining room and kitchen. The dining room was a replica of the dining room found in Woodbury's great-grandfather's house which was destroyed by fire in the early 1800's. Woodbury's wife lived there until her death in 1947, and the house was then given to Historic New England. Her sister lived in the house until 1953.

The historic part of the house is open Friday through Sunday. John Langdon's desk and only a few of his possessions survive. One of the rooms has an exhibit of Portsmouth furniture. The garden is open daily and was created when the addition of the house was made in the early 1900's. It is a large garden with a long arborway with climbing roses and grapes running down the center of the garden. A lawn separates the arbor from a formal garden running the length of the property on the west. On the north end of the lawn, there is a garden house with a porch where one can sit and look back on the house and garden. Behind the garden house, a woodland area with paths flanked by rhododendrons extends back to the next street.

Langdon House - Courtesy of Historic New England

■ MOFFATT-LADD HOUSE AND GARDEN

154 Market Street, Portsmouth, NH 03801
Website: moffattladd.org
Telephone: 603-430-7698
Season: June 1-October 15
Hours and Days of Operation: Monday through Saturday 11-5 PM and Sunday
    1-5 PM-last tour is at 4:30 PM.
Entry Fees: $7 Adults/ $2.50 Children/ Garden Only $2

In the 1700's, Portsmouth, NH was a thriving deepwater port located
on the Piscataqua River as it empties into the Atlantic. English colonists
settled there to take advantage of the river that rarely froze and the timber,
taken from the virgin forests of Maine and so critical to the construction
of the English Naval ships. As a British ship captain, John Moffatt came
to Portsmouth from England to purchase masts for the Royal Navy and
remained to become a very wealthy merchant. In the 1760's, he built
a three story Georgian mansion which faced his wharves with a two-
acre garden behind. It took three years to complete and continues to
be filled with paintings and furniture owned by his descendants. The
house remained in the family until 1912 when it was given to the Colonial
Dames of America in the State of NH.

The house was built as a wedding present for his son, Samuel, who also
became a mercantile merchant. Samuel and his wife, Sarah, lived lavishly
using the mansion as a focus for entertaining. Samuel followed his father
in the mercantile business but was not a good businessman. His record
keeping and informal agreements with other merchants led to disastrous
consequences in 1768 when one of his slave ships sank with all of its cargo.

One of the investors in this venture claimed his financial commitment was a loan, not an investment and sued Samuel for repayment of the loan. Samuel and eventually Sarah fled to the Bahamas to avoid bankruptcy proceedings, leaving two of their children in Portsmouth to be cared for by Samuel's sister, Katherine Moffatt. Katherine moved to the mansion around 1770 and raised her niece and nephew while caring for her ailing father. In the early 1770's, she married William Whipple and had one child who died at 11 months. The Whipples then adopted their niece, Polly, and their nephew left to join his parents in the Bahamas.

Katherine's husband, William Whipple, became involved with activities leading up to the Revolutionary War. He represented New Hampshire at the Continental Congress and was a signer of the Declaration of Independence. He also served as a Brigadier General at Saratoga. Unfortunately, in 1785 he died prematurely at age 54, and one year later his father-in-law, John Moffatt, died. Devastated, Katherine Moffatt continued to live in the mansion. Eventually, after lengthy legal proceedings between Samuel Moffatt's heirs and Katherine, the house was sold to Nathaniel Haven (Polly's husband) who, in 1819, gave the house to his daughter, Maria Ladd. In 1861, after the death of his parents, Alexander H. Ladd took possession of the house and lived there until his death in 1900.

Alexander, a graduate of Phillips Exeter and Dartmouth College, traded in whale oil and cotton. Aware of its historical significance, he was committed to the preservation of the house and refused to move away as the neighborhood around the mansion declined. The gardens were also his passion, and he redesigned the gardens as Colonial Revival Gardens. He brought fill in to create four terraces rising uphill from the rear of the house, and created steps and gravel paths. A series of arbors and pathways connect the terraces and gardens. Alexander kept copious records of his plantings and today, the garden is similar to what was planted over 150 years ago. The garden itself is private, as it is well-encapsulated by the house, the counting house, and the warehouse which dates back to the 1700's. Standing next to the front of the house is a majestic chestnut tree planted by William Whipple which may have come from a chestnut obtained in Philadelphia at the time he signed the Declaration of Independence.

Guided tours of the house, garden, counting house and warehouse take place June through October, seven days a week, and start at the counting house which acts as a visitors center. Tours then move to the Great Hall of the Georgian mansion with its magnificent wallpaper, carved paneling and dentils. The tour of the house includes all three floors. Many of the furnishings and paintings are original to the Moffat family, but in some instances Portsmouth antiques have been added to replace the original ones. Views from the house include the wharves of the Piscataqua River and the garden behind the house.

HAMILTON HOUSE

40 Vaughan's Lane, South Berwick, ME 03908
Website: www.historicnewengland.org and enter zip code
Phone: 207-384-2454
Season: June 1-October 15
Hours and Days of Operation: Wednesday through Sunday; 11-4 PM
House Tours: Wednesday-Sunday: 11-4 PM with last tour at 3 PM
Entry Fees: $10 Adults/ $9 Seniors/ $5 Students

Hamilton House and Gardens is located 13 miles northwest of Portsmouth, New Hampshire in South Berwick, Maine and overlooks the Salmon Falls River which empties into the Piscataqua River and eventually into the Atlantic at Portsmouth. In 1785, Colonel Jonathan Hamilton built a Georgian mansion on a hill called Pipe Stave Point. Hamilton had been born poor in South Berwick in 1745, but at Pipe Stave Point, he built ships, participated in the Triangle Trade, and was a privateer during the Revolutionary War. All these activities made Hamilton a very wealthy man, and his Georgian mansion, which overlooked his shipping empire, was meant to reflect this. After Hamilton's death in 1802, the house and property (about 200 acres) was ultimately purchased by Alpheus Goodwin in 1839. The Goodwin family were farmers and initially prospered by raising sheep (2,000 head). As the price of wool fell, the next generation of Goodwins were forced to sell the farm and mansion in 1895.

Prior to its sale, the house was known as "the Ruins" by townsfolk and was at risk for demolition and the property for development. Sarah Jewett, a neighbor from South Berwick who loved old houses and had frequently visited Hamilton House as a child, stepped in to save the property. Sarah was a highly respected author who socialized with the literary and social elite of Boston. With the help of this literary group, Sarah met Emily Tyson and her step-daughter Elise and convinced them to purchase the property. Widowed by a wealthy husband who had been involved with railroads, Emily bought Hamilton House and 200 acres in 1898 for $4,000, restored the house, and rebuilt and redesigned the gardens using Herbert Browne as the architect for both. Browne changed the face of the house to reflect the Colonial Revival Style, and added porches on the west side of the house. On the east side, he added a kitchen ell and designed a formal and Italianate terraced garden that overlooked the river. At the far end of the garden, a garden cottage with views of the river through French doors was constructed by incorporating the beams and paneling of a nearby Colonial house which was to be demolished. This garden cottage was used for entertaining.

The renovation and furnishing of the house, which was completed in 1900, is now available for viewing by guided tours. Two of the three main rooms on the first floor are decorated with murals by George Porter Fernald, and the woodwork and paneling are exquisite. Filled with early American antiques and Currier and Ives lithographs, the contents of the house are original to Tyson's renovation.

In 1922, Emily Tyson died, leaving her step-daughter to manage the house with her husband Henry Vaughan. Childless, Elise left the house and gardens to Historic New England at her death in 1949. She also left about 200 acres of the adjoining property to the state of Maine as a state park. Under the stewardship of Historic New England, the face of the house has been reworked to appear more Georgian. The garden is also more open, as some of the pergolas were blown down in a storm in the 1950's. However, the garden continues to be maintained, and the Hamilton House grounds are open to the public dawn to dusk.

Hamilton House seen from the Garden-Courtesy of Historic New England

MAINE

Planning a visit to Maine poses a challenge because of the size of the state and its complicated coastline of estuaries, rivers and harbors. There are 6 locations of particular interest in Maine to see. The first is Hamilton House, but due to its proximity to Portsmouth, it has been included in the North Shore section of the book. Four locations are coastal: Thuya, Asticou, Merryspring and Coastal Maine Botanical Gardens are connected by Rte.1 which follows the coastline of Maine from Brunswick to Ellsworth. Therefore, it would seem to be logical to use Rte.1 as the common connector between these four sites. Unfortunately, Rte. 1 is congested and slow-going, so Rte. 95 may make more sense. Asticou, Merryspring, and Coastal Maine Botanical Gardens have no historical houses to visit, but Thuya Garden does. McLaughlin Garden is inland and reached by using Rte. 95 and Rte. 29. The garden is the focus, but the barn and house are open for use as an educational center and a gift shop.

INFORMATION REGARDING DAYS AND HOURS OF OPERATION AS WELL AS FEES AT EACH SITE ARE SUBJECT TO CHANGE AND IT IS BEST TO PHONE OR CHECK THE WEBSITE OF EACH LOCATION FOR UP-TO-DATE INFORMATION

Maine

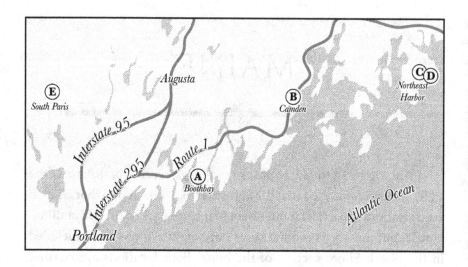

(A) Coastal Maine
Botanical Gardens
132 Botanical Garden Dr,
Boothbay, ME

(B) Merryspring
31 Conway Rd, Camden, ME

(C) Asticou Azalea Garden
Junction of Rte.198 and Rte.3,
Northeast Harbor, ME

(D) Thuya Garden
Thuya Drive (off Rte 3),
Northeast Harbor, ME

(E) McLaughlin Garden
& Homestead
97+103 Main Street,
South Paris, ME

COASTAL MAINE BOTANICAL GARDENS

132 Botanical Garden Drive, Boothbay, ME 04537
Website: www.mainegardens.org
Phone: 207-633-8000
Season: May 1-October 31
Days and Hours of Operation: Daily-9 AM to 5 PM
Tours: Self Guided but Guided tours offered (check website)
Entry Fees: $16 Adults/ $14 Seniors/ $8 Children 3-17/ Under 3-Free

Coastal Maine Botanical Gardens is located on the Back River in Boothbay, Maine. Encompassing 295 acres, it is the largest botanical garden in New England and also the most recent.

In 1991, a grassroots organization of Maine residents was formed to explore the feasibility of creating a botanical garden. After exploring the Maine coast and tidal rivers, the group identified and purchased 128 acres of underdeveloped land with tidal shore frontage in 1996. From 1996 to 2007, a master plan was created and, with the help of volunteers, trails were cleared and gardens were planted. In June 2007, the botanical garden was opened to the public. Prior to its opening, over $8 million had been raised from individuals, foundations and the state of Maine. In 2005, The Gardens was given an additional 120 contiguous acres by the Pine Tree Conservation Society, in 2013 they purchased 22 more acres, and in 2017 they were gifted an additional 25 acres for a total of 295 acres. Since its opening, the older gardens have been upgraded and new gardens have been added. A boat landing with kayaks and a tour boat was added in 2014, making it possible to explore the shoreline of the Back River.

The Gardens is open daily during the summer months from 9 AM-5

PM. Located next to the visitor center and connected by paths and streams, the central gardens are composed of a series of gardens with different themes such as the The Bibby and Harold Alfond Children's Garden, The Woodland Garden or The Lerner Garden of the Five Senses. Peripherally, there are trails that lead to The Giles Rhododendron Garden, the boat landing and other areas of interest. A volunteer shuttle is available to access the more remote parts of the The Gardens, and at the visitor center, visitors may enjoy the cafe which looks out over the gardens.

■ MERRYSPRING NATURE CENTER

31 Conway Road, Camden, ME 04843
Website: www.merryspring.org
Phone: 207-236-2239
Season: Year round
Days and Hours of Operation: Sunrise to sunset
Tours: No regular tours but maps are available in the parking area
Entry Fees: Free

Merryspring is a nature center with a variety of gardens within. Located in both Camden and Rockland, Maine, it encompasses 66 acres of former farmland. Mary Ellen Ross, a resident of Camden and owner of a successful mail-order plant business called "Merry Gardens", was inspired to share her own garden while admiring her backyard garden one September afternoon. After studying other public gardens, Ross and her husband realized their own backyard was insufficient, and they began a search for a property that was large enough to offer a variety of natural experiences. Apparently, a friend found a property that was not for sale, and Ross sought out the owner who agreed to sell the land as a park. Bought with a $70,000 mortgage in the mid 1970's, Ross's dreams were hatched over the ensuing years. The property slowly evolved into a nature center with the help of local volunteers and youth groups. Beginning with the creation of over two miles of hiking trails, the center has gradually evolved with the addition of an arboretum in 1980 and the American Chestnut Breeding Orchard in 1999. A visitor center was created in 1996 to support administrative offices, meeting rooms and a horticultural library.

Upon entering, the property appears to be a nature reserve with trails, meadows, a vernal pool, streams and rolling terrain. Visitors may be surprised to also find gardens, but as might be expected of the owner of a plant mail-order business, multiple gardens were added sequentially over the years. They include an herb garden, day lily garden, rock garden, hosta garden, rose garden, perennial border garden and an annual border garden. The gardens are open daily and maps are available to allow visitors to hike the trails and explore the gardens.

■ ASTICOU AZALEA GARDEN

Junction of Rte.198 and Rte.3 (Peabody Drive), Northeast Harbor, ME. 04662
Website: www.gardenpreserve.org
Phone: 207-276-3727
Season: Early May to End of October
Tours: None but maps are available at gate
Entry Fees: $5 donation suggested per person

In 1604, Samuel De Champlain discovered an island with a range of several mountains that were devoid of trees at their peaks. Due to the barren nature of the mountains, he called this discovery "The Island of the Desert" - later to be named Mount Desert Island. Northeast Harbor is the town on Mount Desert where Asticou Gardens is located.

Northeast Harbor became a resort in the late 1880's when a group of men, "the Rusticators", began to spend their summers there. The "Rusticators" were generally educated, intellectually curious and wealthy men who would spend their summers at the Asticou Inn, where they would be provided three meals a day and a cottage with a beautiful view of the harbor. The inn was owned by the Savage family whose origins in the region dated back to 1790. Originally foresters, farmers, seafarers and fishermen, in the late 1800's they focused their energies on building cottages for this evolving clientele, and the inn was born. Charles Savage (1903-1979) was the third and last generation to run the inn, and he was also the creator of Asticou Azalea Garden and later the garden at Thuya further down the coast. A very curious and artistic child, Charles loved the outdoors and hiking the trails of the inn and Northeast Harbor. In 1922, at the age of 19, his education was interrupted when his father prematurely died, and Charles was called upon to run the inn with his mother. While the inn flourished under his leadership, he continued to pursue artistic interests such as woodcarving and photography. In addition, Charles became a leader of the effort to protect the natural landscape of Mt. Desert and Northeast Harbor. To accomplish this, he enlisted the help of men and women who shared his passion including John D. Rockefeller Jr., Joseph Curtis (creator of the Thuya Estate) and Beatrix Farrand.

In the mid-1950's, Beatrix Farrand, a world-renowned landscape architect, decided to break up her gardens in nearby Bar Harbor, also on Mt. Desert Island. Concerned that this valuable collection of trees, shrubs and plants would be discarded, Savage enlisted the help of Mr. Rockefeller and in 1958, he not only planned but also oversaw the construction of a Japanese-style garden using many of the plants from Mrs. Farrand's garden. The garden was created from a swamp across the street from the inn and completed within a year of its inception. Charles had no training in landscape design, but he had always had a keen interest in Japanese architecture and applied this interest to his design of the new garden at Asticou. The success of Asticou Azalea Garden became the impetus for his leadership in the design and construction of the gardens at Thuya.

The garden is open to the public from sunrise to dusk. One enters Asticou through a gate and onto a gravel pathway that leads through azaleas and rhododendrons to the right and a lawn and a pond to the left. This pond then leads to a stream with criss-crossing bridges and another smaller pond brimming with water lilies. Benches and steps created from boulders found along the Maine coastline are thoughtfully placed, punctuating different areas, gardens, pathways and views throughout. Woodland walks interspersed with randomly arranged flower gardens provide another way of experiencing the beauty of Asticou.

The pond at the entrance to Asticou

THUYA GARDEN AND LODGE

Thuya Drive (off Rte 3), Northeast Harbor, ME. 04662
Website: www.gardenpreserve.org
Phone: 207-276-3727
Season: Late May to mid October
Days and Hours of Operation: Garden is open late May to mid October; Lodge
    is open from mid June to late September 10 AM to 4:30 PM
Entry Fees: $5 donation suggested per person

Thuya Garden (Thuya refers to a species of cedar) and Asticou
Garden share many things in common. Geographically, they both border
the harbor of Northeast Harbor, Maine, a community and harbor on Mt.
Desert Island which is also the home of Acadia National Park. They both,
in part, are the creations of Charles Savage, but in the case of Thuya,
Joseph Henry Curtis (1841-1928) played a more important role.
    Joseph was an only child and at the age of four months, his father died
of tuberculosis. He and his mother then went to live with his maternal
grandparents in Waltham, Massachusetts, where his grandfather was
superintendent of a mill. In 1859 he enrolled at Brown University, but
did not finish because he went off to fight in the Civil War. After the
Civil War, he studied civil engineering at MIT and architecture at Ecole
des Beaux Arts in Paris. In the early 1870's, he went to work for Olmsted,
as a surveyor or civil engineer, on a project to relocate McLean Hospital
in Boston to a more rural setting. During this period, he met the sons
of Charles Eliot who was then president of Harvard. The sons were
outdoorsman and sailors, and their influence led Joseph to Northeast

Harbor which the Eliots, Bishop Doane of Albany and Joseph eventually popularized as a summer colony.

Initially, Curtis stayed with A. C. Savage - a sea captain, fisherman, Civil War veteran and a native to Northeast Harbor. Savage owned an inn on the harbor, and Curtis and his family would spend several weeks a summer there. Sharing experiences of the Civil War and common interests, Savage and Joseph became friends. As a result, in the 1880's Joseph was able to purchase 100 acres of a ridge near Savage's property, where he proceeded to build a series of trails and lookouts that permitted views of the harbor. He also constructed a series of three houses, the last of which is the lodge that today is open to the public and borders the garden. His wife died in 1913, and his only son died in 1918. Beginning in 1909 and continuing to his death in 1928, he created several trusts that transferred ownership of his property to the town of Northeast Harbor, naming Charles Savage, the grandson of A. C. Savage, as the trustee. It was Charles Savage (see Asticou Azalea Garden) who was responsible for the creation of the garden in the 1950's on land that had once been Curtis's orchard.

The garden is open on a daily basis from May 1 - October 31 and the lodge is open from mid June to the end of September. They can be reached by a walking trail from Asticou Garden, switchback trails from the base of Thuya or by Thuya Drive which leads to the front gate of the garden. The contents of the house are original to Curtis's time, and the lodge is rustic, airy and filled with botanical and horticultural books. Visitors enter the garden through wooden gates designed by Charles Savage. Savage designed the garden as a semi-formal garden with drifts of color typical of those designed by Gertrude Jekyll. A grassy pathway runs between the herbaceous beds of the main garden and connects the reflecting pool on the south with a pavilion on the north. The garden is enclosed by borders of azaleas and rhododendrons with paths and gates that lead into the woodland paths which take you to the edge of the ridge with its wonderful views of the harbor and the mountains beyond.

Carved gate at the entrance to Thuya Garden

MCLAUGHLIN GARDEN AND HOMESTEAD

97+103 Main Street, South Paris, ME 04281
Website: www.mclaughlingarden.org
Phone: 207-743-8820
Season: mid May to early October
Hours and Days of Operation: Gift shop and barn open 10-4 PM except
    Mondays. Garden open dawn to dusk.
Entry Fees: Free

The gardens are an oasis of tranquility and greenery in South Paris, Maine. In a sense, it is an urban garden despite the fact that South Paris is a town of only 5,000, nestled between the Sebago Lakes region and the White Mountains to the east. South Paris is located on the Little Androscoggin River, and like many New England towns is a manufacturing and mill town that has lost many of its industries. It was also the home of Hannibal Hamlin, Abraham Lincoln's first vice president, whose family operated a mica mine,

The gardens occupy about four acres and were once a part of a 23 acre farm inherited by Bernard McLaughlin's wife in 1935. Bernard (1898-1995), however, was the gardener of the family. The oldest son of a potato farmer in Limestone, Maine, he graduated from high school as its valedictorian and then went to serve in World War I. He returned to the family farm after the war and helped his family run the farm at a time when potato farming was very profitable. During this period, he not only redesigned the farmhouse, but also created elaborate gardens. With no formal training, he attributed his abilities to his winter job at the Breakers Hotel in Florida, where as a cook, he was able to observe the designs of the gardens at the hotel. When his wife inherited her family farm, Bernard and his wife moved to South Paris. Initially, he worked in the Portland, Maine shipyards and then later at a grocery store in South Paris. His real work, however, was transforming this farm into his passion, a garden in the city.

The design of the garden is considered to be "cottage style", defined as a free-flowing garden where the trees, shrubs, and plants control the design rather than the constraints of walls and steps. Over the next 60 years, Bernard introduced more than 125 species of lilacs and worked with Currier McEwen to hybridize dozens of irises. As a result of his work and expertise in iris propagation, he became President of the American Iris Society. His interest in lilac propagation led him to be one of the founders of the International Lilac Society. A quiet and humble man, he accomplished his dream with only the help of his adopted son, friends and neighbors who wanted to share in his knowledge and love for gardens. In 1995, at the age of 98, Bernard died, leaving no provisions for the preservation of his gardens in his will. The property was about to be sold for development when a group of local folk created a foundation to preserve and perpetuate the garden for the enjoyment of the town and the universe of gardeners.

Today the garden, the house with its gift shop and the barn are open on a daily basis. The allées of lilacs are the central focus of the garden. There is a lush understory of plants ranging from ferns, hosta, phlox and many shade-loving plants surround the lilacs. A woodland path with wildflowers rises up a ridge from a rock garden behind the barn. The plants are well-marked in the main sections of the garden. There is a remarkable selection of plants for sale. Finally, the McLaughlin Foundation and the town have recently acquired the adjoining property with its house and two acres. There are plans to expand the gardens into this area.

McLaughlin Garden

I-89 CORRIDOR (WESTERN NEW HAMPSHIRE AND VERMONT)

With the exception of the Justin Morrill Homestead, the sites in this region were products of the "Gilded Age" although not all of the owners were gilded, but profited from the gains of others. Saint-Gaudens, one of America's great sculptors in the late 1800's, benefitted from the flourishing of American art and architecture that was supported by the wealth of the "Gilded Age" and transformed an old inn overlooking Mt. Ascutney and the Connecticut River into his studio and home. To the south of Saint-Gaudens' estate and in western New Hampshire, John Hay built a summer retreat with 1,000 acres to take advantage of the views of Sunapee Lake and Mt. Sunapee. Further to the west and in Vermont, Robert Lincoln (Abe's son) built an estate that overlooked the Taconic and Green Mountain ranges. To the north near Burlington, Vermont, William Seward Webb (husband of Lila Vanderbilt) transformed 36 farms into a grand summer estate and experimental farm which bordered Lake Champlain with views of the Adirondacks to the west. In central Vermont, near Woodstock, three different families (Marsh, Billings, and Rockefeller) owned and improved the same farm and homestead which looks over the town of Woodstock, the Ottauquechee River, the hills beyond and sits at the base of Mt. Tom. The house of Justin Morrill, a Vermont congressman, senator and originator of the land grant colleges, is located between the Marsh-Billings-Rockefeller farm and Mr. Webb's hideaway on Lake Champlain.

INFORMATION REGARDING DAYS AND HOURS OF OPERATION AS WELL AS FEES AT EACH SITE ARE SUBJECT TO CHANGE AND IT IS BEST TO PHONE OR CHECK THE WEBSITE OF EACH LOCATION FOR UP-TO-DATE INFORMATION

I-89 Corridor
Western New Hampshire and Vermont

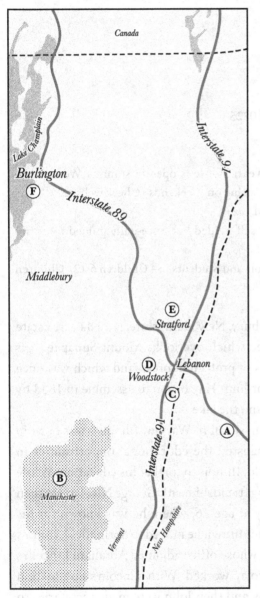

(A) The Fells
456 Route 103A, Newbury, NH

(B) Hildene
1005 Hildene Rd, Manchester, VT

(C) Saint-Gaudens National
Historic Site
139 St Gaudens Rd, Cornish, NH

(D) Marsh-Billings-Rockefeller
National Park
50 Elm St, Woodstock, VT

(E) Morrill Homestead
*214 Justin Morrill Highway,
Strafford, VT*

(F) Shelburne Farms
1611 Harbor Rd, Shelburne, VT

THE FELLS

456 Route 103A, Newbury, NH 03255
Website: www.thefells.org
Phone: 603-763-4789
Season: Grounds are open all year; House is open in summer Wednesday-Sunday and in fall and late spring on Weekends--Check website.
Hours of Operation: 9 AM-5 PM
Tours of the House: Generally self guided but once-daily guided tours are available.Check Website
Entry Fees: $10 Adults/ $8 Seniors and Students/ $4 Children 6-12/ Children 5 and under free

The Fells, located in Newbury, New Hampshire, is an 84 acre estate on the shore of Lake Sunapee which overlooks Mount Sunapee. It is surrounded by over 700 acres of protected forest land which was once part of the summer estate that John Hay began to assemble in 1888 by buying abandoned farms around the lake.

John Hay - the son of a physician in Warsaw, Illinois - was born in 1839 and by age 13 had exhausted the educational opportunities in Warsaw and moved to Pittsfield, Illinois to further his education. While there he developed an enduring friendship with George Nicolay. He then enrolled at Brown University at age 16, where he was known for his debating skills and poetry. After Brown he moved to Springfield, Illinois to read the law with his uncle whose office adjoined Abraham Lincoln's and where his old friend Nicolay worked. With Lincoln's nomination to the presidency, first Nicolay and then John were made secretaries to the campaign, and with Lincoln's ascendancy to the White House, both served as Lincoln's secretaries. Nicolay ran the office and Hay, ever the writer, took responsibility for Lincoln's correspondence. Hay became close to Lincoln and was both a friend, a surrogate son and a resource for Lincoln. Lincoln had such confidence in Hay that he frequently asked him to act as a special emissary despite his age of 22 years.

Following Lincoln's assassination and the end of the Civil War, Hay served abroad: first, in the Paris Legation and then in Vienna and Madrid. His experiences left him a polished diplomat conversant in four languages. In 1870 he returned to the United States and went to work for the New York Tribune as an editorial writer. After two years of enjoying the life of a bachelor, he met Clara Stone. Ten years younger than Hay, she was reserved and had led a protected life as a daughter of a very wealthy Cleveland industrialist. Despite their differences, they were married in February, 1874 and settled in Cleveland where they proceeded to have four children. The marriage brought Hay great financial independence as well as the time to write a successful novel and to complete a 10 volume history of Lincoln in collaboration with Nicolay. Hay also helped run his father-in-law's business, a task that he felt uncomfortable with. In 1879 he was asked to serve as Assistant Secretary of State under Rutherford B Hayes. He accepted this opportunity, given his discomfort with the business world and a desire to move to Washington, a more cosmopolitan city. After his term as Assistant Secretary of State, he served as a guest editor of the New York Tribune where his editorials focused on cleaning up the corruption of Republican politics and carrying on the legacy of his mentor Abraham Lincoln. In 1897 he was made ambassador to England, a role that he cherished in that it allowed him to mix with the intelligentsia and "High Borns" of English society, while maintaining and perpetuating a comfortable relationship between the United States and England. This he accomplished with minimal effort. In the summer of 1898, President McKinley asked Hay to replace his current Secretary of State, a role that he reluctantly accepted, understanding that his responsibilities and workload would be dramatically increased. He served as Secretary under McKinley until his assassination in 1901, and then under Roosevelt until Hay's death on July 1, 1905. Working under Roosevelt was very difficult for Hay since he was a man of peace who had witnessed the tragedies of the Civil War, whereas "T.R." approached international politics with a "big stick" and seemed all too ready to go to war. However, together they gave each other balance and were able to negotiate among other things China's Open Door policy and the Panama Canal treaty.

His time in the State Department did take its toll, and the "Fells" became a place where he would escape in the late summer and early fall. Purchased in 1888, it is located on Lake Sunapee and overlooks Mount Sunapee. Over the years the original farm grew larger by the purchase of adjoining farms so that by 1900, the estate totaled over 1,000 acres. By 1891, the house at the the "Fells" was completed and known by Hay as the "pine shanty". A shanty it was decidedly not, although in 1897, a second house connected by a breezeway, was added for additional space. During John's lifetime the furnishings were simple, and the grounds consisted of rocky pastures and views of the lake and mountain. In 1905 John died, and his son Clarence (1865-1969) inherited the property. Clarence, an archaeologist and curator of archaeology at the Museum of Natural History in New York, and his wife had a strong interest in horticulture. Together they reworked the stoney pastures to accommodate several gardens including the old or woodland garden, the pebble court, the perennial garden, the rose terrace and the rock garden. The main house was restored in 1915 in the Colonial Revival style by the architect Prentice Sanger, and the interior was transformed from simple to stately.

Open to the public from May to October, parking is at the gatehouse where plants from the estate are sold. Visitors walk a quarter-mile to the house down a driveway surrounded by specimen trees and rhododendrons. Tours of the house are generally self-guided, but there is one guided tour daily. A video describing the history of the Fells and the Hay family is also available. Although frequently not original, the furnishings in the house are true to the period. One room is a gallery exhibiting works done by local artists. Tours of the five gardens and trails are also self-guided, but facilitated by very good maps and some interpretative signage. Extensive trails lead along the lake, into the woods and to the wildflower trail. Although trees have grown up since the 1890's, views of Lake Sunapee and the mountains remain beautiful and well worth the visit.

The Fells from the garden-Courtesy of the Fells and Great Island Photo

∎ HILDENE

1005 Hildene Road, Manchester, Vermont 05254
Website: www.hildene.org
Phone: 802-362-1788
Season: Year round
Hours and Days of Operation: Daily-9:30 AM to 4:30 PM
Tours: Generally Self- Guided; Guided Tours available for an additional charge
   (see website)
Entry Fees: $20 Adult/ $5 Youth/ Children under 6 free

Hildene is situated on a hill overlooking a valley and the Battenkill
River below, the Green Mountains to the east and the Taconic Mountain
Range to the west. Hildene (meaning "hill and valley with a stream") lies
outside of Manchester, Vermont where Robert Lincoln chose to establish
the family seat in 1905. Robert was the oldest child of Abraham Lincoln
and the only Lincoln child to survive to adulthood. After graduating from
Harvard Law School, he visited the Equinox Hotel (it is still operating) in
1864 with his mother and younger brother, Tad, for a few weeks during
the summer to escape Washington during its most trying times. After
serving with General Grant at the end of the Civil War and being present
at Appomattox, he started a successful law practice with Edward Isham in
Chicago. Edward was from Bennington, VT, and his family maintained
a residence in Manchester where Robert may have visited and rekindled
his memories of this beautiful state. After one of his visits he returned to
purchase 400 acres to build what was to be the Lincoln ancestral seat for
the next 70 years.

It had been 40 years since his visit to Manchester in 1864. During those intervening years, Lincoln had an impressive career. Besides being a very successful Chicago lawyer, he served as Secretary of War under Presidents Garfield and Arthur. He was also appointed to the Court of St James's as Minister (ambassador to England) by Benjamin Harrison. Robert had no political aspirations and took on these public roles reluctantly and out of a sense of duty. During this 40-year period, on a trip to the Colorado Rockies, he met and befriended George Pullman, the founder of the Pullman Palace Car Company. This relationship made Robert a wealthy man. He became General Counsel of the Pullman Company, and at the death of Pullman in 1897, he became President and then Chairman of the Board until 1924, two years before his death in 1926. At the time of his appointment, the Pullman Company was the largest and most successful manufacturing company on earth.

Robert was 62 when he and his wife, Mary, decided to make Hildene their summer retreat. They hired the architectural firm of Shepley, Rutan and Coolidge (architect of Stanford University and successor firm to H.H. Richardson) to design the house. It was a Georgian Revival style mansion with 24 rooms but was relatively simple compared to most of the great houses built during the "Gilded Age". It was completed in 1905 at a cost of $63,000. The only extravagance of the house was the purchase and installation of an Aeolian organ with more than 900 pipes for $11,000. The grounds were designed by Frederick Todd, a well known Montreal landscape architect and protege of Frederick Law Olmsted.

The Lincolns spent approximately seven out of twelve months at Hildene. For a while, they ran a farm on the property, but after one year, this practice was discontinued because Robert did not have the time to oversee it as he continued to run the Pullman Company. They enjoyed having their children (two daughters and one son) and 3 grandchildren spend summers with them. They had frequent visits from good friends such as William Howard Taft, but avoided entertaining on a large scale. Robert's bedroom was located on the ground floor next to the front door because of arthritis, but also because he liked to step out onto a very long front lawn and hit golf balls. He apparently was a golf fanatic, but not a very good player.

Robert died at age 82 in 1926, and his wife died in 1937, leaving

Hildene to her daughter Mary (their son, known as Jack, had died in Europe at an early age secondary to complications from an infection). Mary died a year later, and left the estate to her niece, Peggy Beckwith, who remained at Hildene until her death in 1975. Peggy was very interested in agriculture and established a dairy farm there. During this period little attention was given to the house and garden. The gardens were allowed to run wild with the privet borders of the parterre garden growing wildly to several feet high.

It was Robert and Mary's wish that Hildene be preserved as a memorial to the Lincoln family, and for this reason, it was left to the Christian Science Church which was unable to appropriately maintain it. Threatened by development, a group of interested neighbors formed a non-profit foundation, "Friends of Hildene" to save it in the late 1970's. Since that time, the house, carriage house, farm and gardens have been restored.

The house contains many of the original furnishings as well as historic memorabilia and paintings. The organ is still there and is played daily for visitors. In one wing of the second floor of the house is an exhibit that honors Abraham Lincoln and focuses on his second inaugural speech. The gardens behind the house have been fully restored and are similar to those in Robert and Mary's time. The parterre garden looks over the mountains and the valley below. With privet hedge borders, each section of the garden contains one color of plant so when in bloom, the garden looks like a stained glass window, particularly when viewed from Mary's sitting room window above. In addition to the formal garden, there is an orchard, cutting garden, miles of trails as well as a goat farm which is open for viewing of milking and cheesemaking. Finally, because of Robert's association with the Pullman Company, visitors may tour a beautifully restored Pullman car.

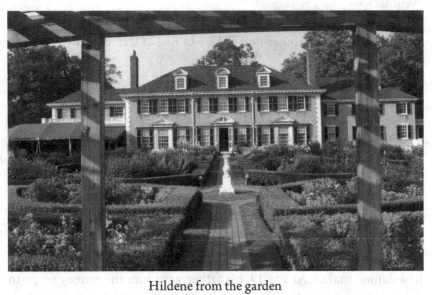

Hildene from the garden

SAINT-GAUDENS NATIONAL HISTORIC SITE

139 Saint Gaudens Road, Cornish, NH 03745
Website: www.nps.gov/saga
Phone: 603-675-2175
Season: House and Exhibits-End of May to End of October; Grounds open
    year round
Days and Hours of Operation: Daily 9 AM to 4:30 PM; Grounds open during
    daylight hours
Tours: See website or phone
Entrance Fees: $10 Adults (16 and over); Children 15 and under-free

Augustus Saint- Gaudens, the son of a French shoemaker and an Irish
mother, was born in Ireland in 1848. The potato famine caused the family
to emigrate to New York City where his father established a successful
cobbler shop selling French shoes. Augustus, the eldest child, showed
great promise in drawing, and by age 13, he excelled as an apprentice
to a cameo maker. At age 19, his father gave him the money to go to
Paris with the hope that Augustus would enroll in the Ecole des Beaux-
Arts, a school which was the training ground for artists from all over the
world. After two years of living in poverty, Augustus was accepted and
enrolled as a student in sculpture. Eventually, he traveled to Italy where
he met his future wife, Augusta, a proper Bostonian and also an artist.
Before Augusta was allowed to marry him, Augustus had to prove his
worthiness as a sculptor by obtaining a major commission. In 1880, he
was commissioned to create a sculpture of Admiral Farragut, a Civil
War hero. A departure from the traditional American style of classical
and idealized sculpture, Augustus's more realistic approach made this

work a major success. After 1883, his career took off and he received more commissions than he could manage. Some of his more well-known sculptures include the Sherman Monument in New York, the Standing Lincoln in Chicago, the Adams Memorial in Washington D.C. and the Shaw Memorial in Boston.,

Augustus and his wife "Gussie" settled in New York City and in 1880, their first child, Homer was born. In the early 1880's Augustus decided to spend the summer in Cornish, New Hampshire and join a summer community of artist friends. Augustus was not a "country boy" but in 1885, he rented an old inn and barn. He had several reasons for doing this: he believed successful men needed a place to go in the summer, and he was also having a secret affair in New York City with one of his models who subsequently bore him another son. In 1892, he bought the inn, added onto it and transformed the adjoining acres into gardens and recreation areas which included a bowling green, a swimming pool and a golf course. Although Saint-Gaudens was diagnosed with cancer in 1900, he continued to work producing public sculptures and reliefs. As his health and energy diminished, he moved to Cornish and acted as an executive sculptor, overseeing the planning and implementation of this work until his death in 1907.

After his death, Gussie and her son Homer continued to summer in Cornish, and in 1919, they established the Saint-Gaudens Memorial protecting the house and surrounding estate as a public historic site. In 1965, the site was donated to the National Park Service.

The house is situated on a hillside that once allowed for views of Mount Ascutney and the Connecticut River. Today the view of the river is obscured by tree growth, but the view of the mountain is still inspiring. The house with its original contents is open to the public by guided tours daily from June to October. Visitors may view a gallery of his work and his studio with its interpretative signage. A video on Saint-Gaudens life and work is on view at the visitor's center, and the grounds of the estate are breathtaking. The area around the house is bordered by a series of garden rooms defined by 10 foot white pine and hemlock hedges. One garden room contains a copy of the "Shaw Memorial" and another the "Adams Memorial". The northern border of the hedge forms an allée of birches and carries the eye to the fields and Mount Ascutney beyond. Off the kitchen lies an enclosed cutting garden, and between the porch of the house and the studio is a sunken, formal Italian Garden. A grape arbor provides shade over the porch on the south side of the studio and on the east is a sunken terrace with marble benches shaded by birches. The gardens are living galleries punctuated by a lifetime of works by Saint -Gaudens.

"Aspet"-Saint Gaudens Residence

■ MARSH-BILLINGS-ROCKEFELLER NATIONAL HISTORIC PARK

50 Elm Street, Woodstock, VT 05091
Website: www.nps.gov/mabi
Phone: 802-457-3368 x22
Season: Late May to End of October; Trails and Grounds open year round
Days and Hours of Operation: Daily -10 AM to 5 PM
House Tours: Daily- 10 AM to 5 PM
Entrance Fees: $8 Ages 16-61 / $4 Ages 62 and over / Free 15 and under

Nestled at the base of Mount Tom in Woodstock, Vermont, this house and garden overlook the 200 year old farm owned by three different families, the town of Woodstock and the Ottauquechee River. These three families were all similar, not only in their love for this land, but also for their contribution to the protection of the place, as well as their commitment to the protection of natural resources all over the world.

George Marsh was born on this property in 1801 and moved to a smaller version of the present mansion in 1806. He was a voracious reader, but at age 7, because of failing eyesight, he turned his energies to the outdoors and developed a tremendous appreciation and knowledge of the natural world. Marsh became very concerned about the deforestation of the hills and valleys and its effect on the erosion of Vermont's soils, flooding of waterways and the consequent loss of fishing and productive farming. He regained his sight, went to Dartmouth College, served in the U.S. Congress, and ultimately was U.S. Minister to Turkey and Italy. On his travels through Turkey, Marsh saw the effect of centuries of man's abuse of the land which he described as a "worn-out wasteland". While ambassador to Italy in the 1860's, he wrote *Man and Nature,* the first book to address the need for man to protect nature as a step toward protecting the environment. While George was in Italy, his family's homestead was sold to Frederick Billings in 1869.

Frederick was a Woodstock boy, but at age 25, went to California to seek his fortune. With the recent discovery of gold, Billings became very successful as a lawyer, settling land claims and dabbling in real estate. At the onset of the Civil War, he left California with some regret as he had come to love the beauty and resources of California where he became interested in protecting the Yosemite Valley. He moved to New York City where he became president of the Northern Pacific Railroad. In 1869, having decided to move home to Woodstock with his wife and four children, Billings enlarged and transformed the Marsh's Federal Style house to a Queen Anne mansion. Expanding the farm to encompass 2,000 acres, Billings began a period of reforestation of the hills and valleys around him. In doing so, he employed over 100 men in the Woodstock area at a time when families were leaving Vermont because the depleted soil could no longer support them. Billings also introduced the latest agricultural techniques and shared them with his neighbors. In gratitude for his good fortune, he dedicated himself to restoring the farming potential of Vermont through good conservation techniques.

Billings died in 1890, and his wife, daughters and granddaughters carried on his work until 1954. In 1934, Mary French, his granddaughter, married Lawrence Rockefeller, son of John D. Rockefeller Jr. Mary and Lawrence shared a love for Woodstock, the farm and a commitment to the preservation of the environment. Like his father, Lawrence worked with the National Park Service to establish national parks. As an entrepreneur, he worked to create recreational opportunities through access to areas of beauty (e.g. The Rock Resorts). Mary and Lawrence carried on the work of Mary's grandfather, and in 1992, they donated the house and over 500 acres to the National Park Service. Previously, they had created a separate foundation to operate the farm and educate the public about the methods and practice of agriculture.

Open to the public with regular tours, the mansion has furnishings and paintings original to Frederick Billings' time. The art collection includes many fine landscapes by well known artists (Albert Bierstadt, William Bradford). The house is a historic house-museum, as there is definite evidence of the Rockefellers' time there with their modern conveniences. The views from the house on the hill look down over the valley to the farm, the Ottauquechee River to the east and Woodstock to the south. The large, well-marked garden has terraces that ascend from the house to the greenhouses and eventually to a system of carriage trails built by Frederick Billings that lead up over Mount Tom. If you have the energy to make the hike, it is well worth it, as you will encounter fields with grazing cows, streams, a pond and wonderful views.

Billings Mansion

SENATOR JUSTIN MORRILL HOMESTEAD

214 Justin Morrill Highway, Strafford, VT 05072
Website: www.historicsites.vermont.gov
Phone: 802-765-4484
Season: End of May to Mid October
Days and Hours of Operation: Wednesday through Sunday Plus Holiday
    Mondays 11 to 5
Days of House Tours: Same as above-tours given hourly
Entrance Fees: $6 Adults/ Children 14 and under - Free

In 1810 Justin Morrill was born into a family of 10 children in the town of Strafford, Vermont. His father was a blacksmith and couldn't afford to educate Justin beyond the age of 15 despite Justin's obvious intellect and curiosity. After he apprenticed in a general store, Justin opened and owned several stores of his own which allowed him to retire in 1848 at the age of 38. With the idea of building an experimental farm and a homestead for his future family, he purchased 100 acres in Strafford. Drawing on the ideas of Andrew Jackson Downing, he built a Gothic house, created gardens and erected several barns that would specifically house horses, cows and sheep, etc. On the completion of the house, he married Ruth Swan, a schoolteacher, and proceeded to have children. His first child died and his son James was born in 1857.

In 1854, Justin was persuaded to run for Congress and won, leading to a long career as a legislator. He served in the U.S. House of Representatives until 1867 when he moved to the U.S. Senate. Initially, Ruth and James stayed in Strafford with her sister Louise while Justin served in Washington, but in 1876, the family built a mansion in

Washington and spent six months of the year there while Congress was in session. However, every summer they would return to Strafford. Justin started out as a Whig, but given his strong abolitionist views, became a Republican in the late 1850's. He believed in the gold standard and tariffs as a way of strengthening and building U.S. business (Morrill Tariff). He is best remembered for his championship of legislation that allowed governmental support of public non-military colleges or land grant colleges where the curriculum would focus on agricultural and mechanical studies. These bills, passed in 1872 and revised in 1890, led to the creation of 105 colleges and universities in the U.S. (including Cornell, MIT, LSU, UVM, Rutgers, Purdue, etc). Justin served in the Senate until his death in 1898.

His son James continued to occupy the house in Strafford until he died in 1910, and it was then occupied by Ruth's sister until her death in 1919. The house was then purchased as a summer retreat in 1936. Understanding its historical significance, the new owner did very little structurally to change the house. In 1964, the state of Vermont took possession of the house to be maintained as a historic museum.

The house and the outbuildings are open for tours Wednesday through Sunday. Many of the furnishings of the house are original including Morrill's library. In the carriage house, there is a very good exhibit detailing Morrill's life along with a demonstration of equipment used back in the 1850's. Morrill designed the gardens, grounds and the house. In front of the house, there is a formal garden with serpentine paths, mature shrubs and Arabesque flower beds, and many of the trees planted by Morrill are over 150 years old. Behind the house are the kitchen gardens (used by the University of Vermont as experimental gardens) and terraces that lead up to the barns and remnants of the orchard. From the hill where the house and farm buildings stand, one can see the tip of the steeple emanating from Town Hall in Strafford.

SHELBURNE FARMS

1611 Harbor Road, Shelburne, VT 05482
Website: www.shelburnefarms.org
Phone: 802-985-8686
Season: Grounds and Store-Year Round: Tours of the House and Barn-Mid
    May to mid October
Days and Hours of Operation: Daily-9AM to 5:30 PM
Days of Tours: Variable-Several Tours are offered, Check Website or Phone
Entry Fees: $8 Adults/ $6 Seniors/ $3 Children (3-17); Additional Fees for
    Tours - see Website

Now owned by a nonprofit foundation whose mission is to promote
a conservation ethic that leads to a healthy and sustainable use of land,
Shelburne Farms is a 1400-acre estate located on the east side of Lake
Champlain just south of Burlington, Vermont. It Is an active farm with
over 120 dairy cows, sheep, gardens and woodlands. Annually, the dairy
produces over 160,000 pounds of cheese, and the woodlands produce
timber and over 600 gallons of maple syrup. It is also the home of the
Shelburne Inn, the former summer home of the Webb family.

Its genesis dates back to 1881 when William Seward Webb (1851-
1926) married Lila Vanderbilt (1860-1936). Webb, the son of an editor
of a New York newspaper, graduated from Columbia Medical School
in 1875 and practiced as a surgeon for a short time, but sought a more
lucrative career to gain the approval of his future father-in-law, William
Vanderbilt (son of Cornelius and then one of the richest men in the
United States). Dr. Webb started his own Wall Street investment firm,
and then transitioned into the railroad business and the ownership of the

Wagner Palace Car Company which eventually merged with the Pullman Car Company (the largest corporation in the United States in the late 1800's). His marriage to Lila in 1881 coincided with William's discovery of the beauty of Lake Champlain while traveling on railroad business. The couple made the decision to create a country estate along the shores of Lake Champlain as an escape for the family from their winter home on Park Avenue in New York City. Because farming was on the decline in Vermont in the late 1800's, the Webbs also hoped to introduce to Vermont the most modern agricultural techniques. Depleted soil due to poor farming practices, a better lifestyle offered by working in factories and competition from much bigger and more efficient farms in the West, all contributed to the decline of farming in Vermont. Dr. Webb wanted to help these fleeing farmers, but he also took advantage of their disenchantment with Vermont agriculture by purchasing 36 farms for a total of 3800 acres along the shore of Lake Champlain.

The Webbs hired Frederick Law Olmsted to create a park-like estate with rolling grasslands interspersed with woodlands and crisscrossed by winding roads and trails that would optimize the view of the lake, the main house and countryside. The overall plan called for the demolition of the 36 existing farm houses and their outbuildings, walls and fences to be followed by the construction of new housing and barns. Robert Robertson (the architect of Hammersmith Farm and Ballantyre) was hired, and over the years he designed 36 structures at Shelburne Farms which included the following: the main house built in 1885; an addition in 1899 enlarging the entire house to 100 rooms; the 5 story farm barn - the largest barn in the U.S. at the time it was built; the horse breeding barn with over 100 stalls and the largest riding indoor ring in the U.S. before 1939; the coach and the dairy barn. Two hundred fifty workers were needed to support the farm and the activities of the family.

Maintenance of the estate became more difficult around 1913 with the introduction of the income and real estate taxes as well as the increasing cost of labor due to competition from factory jobs. The Webbs' hope was that the farm would be self-sustaining from revenues derived from its agricultural activities, but this never occurred. In 1926 Dr. Webb died of complications of rheumatoid arthritis, and in 1936 Lila died.

Following her death, the house and the core farm with its barns were purchased by Vanderbilt Webb, her youngest son, and subsequent to that, by his son Derek Webb. Derek ran the farm from 1938 until his death in 1984. In the late 1960's, Derek and his six children, faced with the high cost of running the farm, had to choose between running the farm as a public nonprofit enterprise or selling it for development. They chose the former, and at Derek's death the property was turned over to Shelburne Farms Resources in 1984.

Largely unoccupied since 1936, the main house with its 24 bedrooms has been restored, and in 1987, it was opened to the public for tours and also as a restaurant and an inn. The barns continue to be used for various purposes including environmental education, cheesemaking, concerts, conferences and furniture production.

General tours of the estate are available on a daily basis and include the main house, the farm barn, the grounds and the gardens. The general tour includes only a few of the rooms on the first floor of the main house, now the Inn at Shelburne Farms. Visitors to the coach barn will see the cheese production facility. There are also specific tours of the house and gardens offered two times a week. This specific tour of the house and garden includes a tour of the second and third floors and all of the first floor rooms. About 75% of the furnishings of this Queen Anne mansion are original. Behind the main house, the terraced garden extends down to a cliff and a balustrade that overlooks Lake Champlain and the Adirondacks to the west. Recently restored at a cost of $3 million, the Italianate gardens largely reflect Lila's design of the garden in 1912. Finally, there are 10 miles of trails on the estate, and these can be explored without a guide.

Entrance view of the main house at Shelburne Farms

THE BERKSHIRES

The Berkshires are located in western Massachusetts and lie east of the Hudson River Valley. The name, Berkshires, refers to the range of mountains that dominates the area and extends south from Vermont's Green Mountains. The Housatonic River flows through the area, and in the 1750's, allowed for the original settlements, which subsisted on farming, sawmills, and textiles. Because of the area's beauty, its accessibility to New York City and Boston and the advent of train service, artists and writers began to visit in the 1840's. In the 1880's, the super rich of the "Gilded Age" came to the area and began to build large estates in the Berkshire Cottage Period.

The houses were large and their gardens extensive. Interestingly, the owners of the houses on this tour were different from their neighbors in that most were not captains of industry: one was a sculptor (Daniel Chester French at Chesterwood); another was a writer (Edith Wharton at the Mount); and a third was an Egyptologist at Ashintully. A corporate lawyer and eventually minister to the Court of St. James, only Joseph Choate at Naumkeag adhered to the normal stereotypic owner of the "Gilded Age".

The other site in the area is the Berkshire Botanical Garden that was built in the 1920's with land, labor (their gardeners) and expertise donated by the ladies of the "Gilded Age". The towns in the area, Lenox, Stockbridge and Lee, are old, well maintained and have avoided the scourge of sprawl. The countryside is enchanting with its hills, marshes, rolling fields and waterways.

Also included in this section of the book is Tower Hill Botanical Garden. Tower Hill actually lies between the Boston region and the Berkshires, just north of Boston in Boylston, Massachusetts. However, it is not far from the highway which connects the Berkshires and Boston and well worth the visit.

INFORMATION REGARDING HOURS AND DAYS OF OPERATION AS WELL AS FEES AT EACH SITE ARE SUBJECT TO CHANGE AND IT IS BEST TO PHONE OR CHECK THE WEBSITE OF EACH LOCATION FOR UP-TO-DATE INFORMATION.

Berkshires

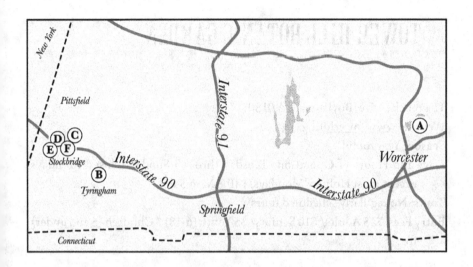

(A) Tower Hill Botanic Garden
11 French Dr, Boylston, MA

(B) The Mount
2 Plunkett Street, Lenox, MA

(C) Chesterwood
4 Williamsville Rd, Stockbridge, MA

(D) Naumkeag
6 Prospect Hill Rd, Stockbridge, MA

(E) Berkshire Botanical Garden
5 W Stockbridge Rd, Stockbridge, MA

(F) Ashintully
Sodem Rd, Monterey, MA

TOWER HILL BOTANIC GARDEN

11 French Drive, Boylston, MA 01505
Website: www.towerhillbg.org
Season: Year round
Days and Hours of Operation: Tuesday through Sunday (closed Mondays
    except most Holiday Mondays) ; 10 AM to 5 PM
Tours: No regularly scheduled tours
Entry Fees: $15 Adults/ $10 Seniors/ $5 Youth (6-18) / Children (5 and under)
    free

Located in Boylston, Massachusetts, a few miles north of Worcester,
Tower Hill is the site of the headquarters of the Worcester County
Horticultural Society as well as the site of its botanical garden. The
third oldest in the country, the Horticultural Society was founded by
24 men with an interest in horticulture, but whose occupations ranged
from merchants, public officials and professionals. In 1840, they entered
a fruit and flower display at the annual cattle show of the Worcester
Agricultural Society. Their efforts were well-received and, as a result,
the Horticultural Society was incorporated in 1844.. Modeled on Great
Britain's Royal Horticultural Society, its mission was to advance the
science of horticulture and to encourage and improve its practice.

Worcester became a major industrial city with great wealth in the
late 1840's. For the next 100 years, both the city and the Horticultural
Society flourished and carried out its mission by holding regular
horticultural shows. The success of these shows and activities required
larger horticultural halls, the last of which was constructed in 1928. With
the advent of the Depression and World War II, the prosperity of the city

declined, and with this decline, some of the great, outlying estates scaled back their gardens and had less to contribute to horticultural activities in the city. With this sociologic and economic shift in mind, the Board of the Horticultural Society decided to pursue its mission of education and scientific advancement by constructing a botanical garden and selling their horticultural hall in Worcester. After searching for several years, they located a 120-acre dairy farm in Boylston, Massachusetts and purchased it in 1986.

The farm sits on a hill and has exquisite views of Mount Wachusett and the valley below filled by the Wachusett Reservoir. Although not open to the public, the original farmhouse, dating back to the 1720's, serves as a backdrop to four gardens: 1) the cottage garden, immediately adjacent to the farmhouse, is small and a source of ideas for one's own garden 2) the vegetable garden, full of color and unusual vegetables 3) the great lawn, a gathering place for functions at the botanical garden containing 350 species and varieties of woody trees and shrubs interspersed with perennials and annuals and 4) the secret garden, which contains plants which are more tolerant of wet soil.

The farm's dairy barn was moved to Hingham, Massachusetts to make room for two large conservatories as well as the education and visitor's center. The education center contains a comprehensive horticultural library, exhibits of plants, a gift shop and a restaurant which takes advantage of the views of the Wachusett Reservoir. In the winter, the conservatories house camellias, begonias, a citrus collection and other plants. Lying between the two conservatories, the winter garden highlights winter hardy plants with interesting bark, leaves or berries. Plants from the conservatories are moved outside in summer, and the winter garden is transformed into a garden one might find in an Italian village with potted plants, a central fountain and statuary.

Beyond the conservatories lies the systematic garden, an educational garden where plants are grouped into 28 families. "Pliny's allée" leads to a three-mile long network of trails to overlooks and to woodland gardens interspersed with statuary and temples. Along the trails, visitors will discover the wildlife garden, a pond, a shade garden and finally, the orchard with its 119 species of apple trees.

THE MOUNT - EDITH WHARTON'S HOME

2 Plunkett Street, Lenox, MA 01240
Website: www.edithwharton.org
Phone: 413-551-5111
Season; May- February
Hours and Days of Operation: Open daily from 10-5 PM from May to October;
    open Saturdays and Sundays November through February
Days and Hours of House Tours: check website
Entry Fees: $18 adults/$17 seniors / 18 and under free / $10 military discount

The Mount, built by Edith Wharton and her husband Teddy in 1902, is located in Lenox, Massachusetts in the Berkshires. At that time, Lenox was known "as the inland Newport" as it attracted the super rich of the "Gilded Age" who built large estates with large villas. Like Newport it was a very social place, but Lenox appealed to people seeking an intellectual community and a place where one might find some degree of privacy. Those aspects of Lenox attracted Edith and her husband in their search to find a replacement for their summer house in Newport known as "Land's End".

In 1901, the Whartons bought a 113 acre farm overlooking the rolling terrain that sloped down to Laurel Lake. To design the house, Edith engaged Ogden Codman, an up-and-coming Boston architect who had collaborated with Edith on a very successful book on interior design. Possessing her own ideas of design, Edith was very involved with the planning and construction of the house. She was a demanding client, and at some point during the construction, excessive costs led her to fire Codman and hire Frances Hoppin, the architect of Ashintully and

Blithewood. The house was built with a limited budget. The Whartons were rich, but they had to be careful with their money. They ultimately built the 16,850 square-foot house for $57,000 at a time when some of the "Gilded Age" mansions were built for $2 million. In 1902, at age 40, Edith moved into her new summer house with her husband. The house seemed more hers than his because she had been totally involved with the planning of both the house and garden. Also, the purchase of the property and construction of the house were made possible by Edith's inherited family money and the sale of the Wharton's Newport property. Profits from Edith's successful 1905 novel, "House of Mirth", helped build the gardens.

Childless, Edith settled into a routine of writing in the early morning while in bed, and then gardening in the afternoon and pursuing social activities such as horseback riding or motoring with her friends, often other writers and artists. She continued to summer at The Mount for the next 9 years, arriving in early spring and leaving in late autumn. During this period, her relationship with her husband deteriorated. Married when Edith was 23, Teddy and Edith had never been a good match. She was 12 years younger and an intellectual while he was a sportsman. As the years went by, Teddy's behavior became more erratic, using money from Edith's trust funds to go off on "spending sprees", while also having indiscrete affairs. In retrospect, he was probably bipolar, and ultimately, this led to the collapse of the marriage and their decision to sell "The Mount" in 1911. Edith then moved to France for the rest of her life and published over 40 books in 40 years.

After the Wharton's departure, the estate was owned by two different families until 1942, when it was sold to Foxhollow School for $18,000. A girls' school, Foxhollow bought the house primarily for its stables, but used the house as a dormitory until 1976 when the school closed. It was later bought by the Edith Wharton Foundation which began a restoration of the property in 1997. To date, over $10 million has been spent on the restoration of the house, gardens and grounds.

Visitors approach the house by way of a long meandering driveway through the woods and under an allée of sugar maples. The woods are carpeted with ferns and vinca which pick up the shadows and sunlight filtering through the trees. This approach to the property was designed by Edith's niece, Beatrix Farrand, who was a landscape architect. Edith designed the more formal gardens at the rear of the house. From the house on the hill, a series of terraces leads down to the gardens and eventually to the lake. To the left side of the terraces there is a French flower garden and to the right an Italian walled garden. Separating the two gardens is a long allée made up of sculpted linden trees and by a gravel path.

The house itself is sunlit and colorful in contrast to the Victorian heaviness of many houses of that era. The design of the house maximizes the views of the landscape with French doors that open onto the terrace overlooking the gardens. Most of the house furnishings are not original but are appropriate to Edith's time, since she moved away after living there only 9 years. However, the library does contain her collection of books. Several rooms on the second floor are not furnished, but they contain exhibits that focus on Edith's life and work as well as the story of the estate. There are daily house and garden tours. Times are posted on the website (www.edithwharton.org).

The Mount looking from the gardens

CHESTERWOOD

4 Williamsville Road, Stockbridge, MA 01262
Website: www.chesterwood.org
Phone: 413-298-3579
Season: Memorial Day Weekend through Columbus Day Weekend
Hours and Days of Operation: Daily - 10 AM to 5 PM
Tours: Self Guided (House closed from 12:30 PM to 2 PM)
Entry Fees: $18 Adults / $17 Seniors / Free -Children under 13

Located in Stockbridge, Massachusetts, Chesterwood, a National Trust Historic Site, is the country home, studio and garden of Daniel Chester French. French (1850 - 1931) was America's greatest sculptor of public monuments, best known for his masterpiece, the Lincoln Memorial in Washington, D.C.. Daniel was born in Exeter, New Hampshire but moved with his family to Cambridge and ultimately Concord, Massachusetts. Never much of a student, he preferred whittling to math and physics, and spent as much time as possible in the woods of Concord. After a brief and unsuccessful time at the Massachusetts Institute of Technology, he moved back to Concord where the town selectmen chose him to do a memorial honoring the Minutemen of the American Revolution. When the statue was completed in 1875, French gained national acclaim for the energy and spirit of this work. He then went to Italy to study for a year, and on upon his return in 1876, his work generated more interest. This interest may have been fueled by the fact that his father, a lawyer, judge and Undersecretary of the Treasury, was in a position to introduce French to influential patrons at a time when American architecture was undergoing a renaissance. With the design and construction of new public buildings came a demand for sculpture. Examples of newly constructed public buildings during this period included the Boston Post Office, the St. Louis Post Office, the Philadelphia Post Office and Courthouse, and later on, the Boston Public Library and the New York Custom House. French collaborated with the architects of all of these magnificent buildings to adorn them with allegorical sculptures.

In 1888, French married his first cousin, Mary French, and worked in his studios in Concord and New York City. In the summers of 1891 to 1893, he and Mary stayed in Cornish, New Hampshire at the farm of his fellow sculptor, Augustus Saint-Gaudens. As a result of this visit to the country, he began to look for property in Stockbridge, Massachusetts, and in 1896, he purchased an 80-acre farm with views of pastures and Monument and Everett Mountains beyond. Initially, he constructed a studio, designed by Henry Bacon, an architect that he had collaborated with at the Chicago's World's Fair. He, his wife and one daughter, Margaret, lived in the old farmhouse. After a few years, he again hired Henry Bacon to build a larger house that French described as a Colonial Revival.

French designed the grounds of the property. It was his intent to make the property self-sufficient, and he had livestock, orchards and gardens. His interest in farming came from both his own childhood experiences on the family farm as well as his father's interest in farming and horticulture. A childhood friend accused him of sculpting the earth because French had such a desire to "tame" the landscape.

While in Italy, French had met and worked with two artists whose studios were situated in formal gardens. This inspired him to do the same at Chesterwood. On one side of his studio a porch overlooks the pastures and mountains. On the other side, French designed a partially enclosed garden that had an axial relationship with the studio. The studio was divided into three parts: on the south was the working side; on the west a room for casting; and on the north, a more formal area where French would entertain guests and clients. Immediately outside the formal part of the studio was the garden with a sitting area that was half enclosed by an exedra (a rounded marble bench) backed by a privet hedge. A fountain, designed by French, is placed in the center of this area. From the marble bench, long gravel paths with abutting garden beds extend extend east, west and north. These paths gradually merge into woodland paths that eventually lead to woodland "outdoor rooms" or to a lookout over the valley.

French loved designing his gardens and he also enjoyed designing gardens for friends and neighbors free of charge. Very involved with the work of gardening and maintaining his trails, he returned to Chesterwood each spring with great anticipation to see what nature had brought forth from the previous year.

Chesterwood is a beautiful place, and at the visitor's center (the old barn), an exhibit details French's life and sculpture. Tours of the house, garden and studio are self-guided, but docents are on hand to answer questions. Site interpreters are available in each of the buildings, and many of French's works are on view in the studio and barn. A detailed map allows visitors to explore the gardens and trails. Group tours to Chesterwood are available by advanced registration only.

French's Studio and Garden

■ NAUMKEAG

6 Prospect Hill Road, Stockbridge, MA 01262
Website: www.thetrustees.org
Phone: 413-298-8138
Season: End of May through Columbus Day; The estate is also open several
    weekends before and after the regular season - check website or call for
    specifics.
Days and Hours of Operation: Daily during the regular season 10 AM to 5 PM
Entrance Fees: $15 Adults / Children up to 12 - Free

    Naumkeag is a product of the "Gilded Age" and was built in 1884 by
Joseph Choate and his wife, Caroline, in Stockbridge, Massachusetts.
Longtime visitors to the Berkshires, the Choates were interested in
creating a summer retreat for their family, and not a showpiece of wealth,
the norm of their newly rich neighbors. They purchased 48 acres, hired
Charles McKim to design a house, and at the the end of one year, a 44-
room retreat was ready for occupancy. Extensive gardens were created
that took advantage of the views of the farm and the mountains beyond.
    It was Joseph Choate's success as one of America's first corporate
lawyers that allowed all this to happen. Born in 1832 in Salem,
Massachusetts to a physician, he attended Harvard and Harvard Law
School, and then moved to New York City where he successfully defended
the corporate interests of the monopolies being created after the Civil
War. In 1894, he successfully argued against the provisions of the Income
Tax Law of 1874, and effectively derailed the use of the income tax as
a source of revenue until 1913. A Republican, he ran unsuccessfully
for the U,S. Senate in 1895. In 1899, he was appointed to succeed John

Hay as the Minister to the Court of St. James, and there, among other accomplishments, he was successful in negotiating the Hay-Pauncefote Treaty which allowed for the construction of the Panama Canal.

Joseph died in 1917, and Caroline continued to summer at Naumkeag until her death in 1929. The estate was left to their daughter, Mabel, and in a sense, Naumkeag then entered a new era. Although she never married, she was very active in entertaining family and friends. She was artistic like her mother, and traveled frequently, bringing treasures back to Naumkeag. In the late 1920's, she met Fletcher Steele at a Lenox Garden Club function. This chance encounter led to the transformation of Naumkeag's grounds over the next 30 years, since Mr. Steele was a landscape architect who, at that time, was considered to be a leading innovator in this field. Having studied under Frederick Law Olmsted, Jr. at Harvard, his architecture and garden design had evolved from a more traditional and classical style to one which embraced an Art Deco style. Together, Mabel and Fletcher recreated several new gardens at Naumkeag using the bones of the old garden and always maintaining the views. Often, these gardens were inspired by their frequent travels, such as to China, as well as by their desire to incorporate travel artifacts into these gardens. The "Moongate" was the last of the structures to be incorporated into the gardens. At that time, in consultation with Fletcher Steele, Mabel realized that if she wanted to preserve the house and gardens in their completed state, that she would have to leave Naumkeag to an organization willing to take on that role. Accordingly, at her death, Naumkeag was left to The Trustees with an endowment to maintain it.

The "shingle-style house" and gardens are open daily during the summer. Tours of the house are guided and last about one hour. The contents of the house are original and include portraits of Mabel and her mother by John Singer Sargent and a bust of Joseph by Saint-Gaudens. The furniture is Louis XV style, and there are extensive collections of books, Chinese porcelain and Delft china.

Tours of the gardens are self-guided, but audio tours are available and helpful. There are occasional guided tours of the gardens. Olmsted was chosen as the original landscape architect, but was fired because his design sited the house in a location of a favorite oak tree that the

Choates wanted to preserve. The house location was then moved up the hill, preserving the oak and improving the views. In the 1880's, Nathan Barrett then took over the grounds and gardens design which was more formal than the design which Mabel and Fletcher Steele undertook from 1926 until 1958. The gardens at Naumkeag are extensive, varied and take time to fully appreciate. They include: a rose garden, an evergreen garden, a peony tree display garden, an afternoon garden room with objects obtained from Mabel's travels and a walled Chinese garden. Construction of the Chinese Garden took 30 years and contains a temple and a pool. Other notable features are 2 allées: one bordered by Linden trees and the other by arbor vitae. Most notable is Steele's unique design of the "Blue Steps" with its four fountains and covering of birches leading down to a delphinium and cut flower garden at the bottom of the hill. Views from the house and garden encompass a pastoral scene with grazing cows in the valley below and the distant mountains beyond.

Front entrance to Naumkeag

■ ASHINTULLY

Sodem Road, Tyringham, MA
Website: www.thetrustees.org
Season: Early June to mid October
Days and Hours of Operation: Wednesday and Saturday, 1-5 PM Only
Tours: No regularly scheduled tours but Barn and Studio are open
Entry Fees: Free

Ashintully (Gaelic for "brow of the hill") is located in Tyringham, Massachusetts, 10 miles southeast of Stockbridge. In 1903, Robb de Peyster Tytus and his newlywed wife, Grace, spent their honeymoon riding through the Tyringham Valley. Over the next few years, they purchased four farms and established a working farm of over 1,000 acres. After living in one of the farmhouses for a few years, Tytus, an Egyptologist and an heir to the Tytus fortune, started the construction of a house that overlooked the Tyringham Valley. He hired Francis Hoppin (see the Mount and Blithewood) to design the house. It took three years for the construction to be completed and cost $1 million (the Mount cost $57,000. The house contained 35 rooms, 10 bathrooms, and a library that measured 75 feet long by 32 feet wide by 32 feet high. Although made of stucco composed of Nantucket sands, the house was known as the "Marble Palace" and was a Georgian-style mansion fronted by four Doric columns.

Shortly after the house was completed in 1913, Tytus died of tuberculosis at age 37, leaving two daughters. His wife, Grace, remarried and bore a son, John McLennan, in 1915. Grace was divorced from John's father soon after, and over the ensuing years, John and his sisters spent many happy summers there. At the death of their mother, his two sisters inherited the property but decided to sell it. At the prodding of friends and neighbors who were concerned that the property would be developed and timbered, John, at age 22, purchased the estate in 1937 from his two sisters and moved to Tyringham. In the winter, he lived in the farmhouse and in the summer, he moved to the Marble Palace. He married, had two daughters and became a well-respected composer of chamber music for piano and organ. He converted the barn next to the farmhouse into his studio which is now open to the public.

In the early 1950's, the Marble Palace became too expensive to maintain and John decided to sell it. While in the process of emptying the mansion, a brush fire spread to the house and it burned down. Only the foundation and four Doric columns remain. One can climb up the hill through John's gardens and follow a woodland trail leading to what was once the front terrace and gaze through the Doric columns over Tyringham Valley.

In the 1960's, John designed and built a garden behind the farmhouse that ascends a hill to a woodland trail that leads to the ruins of the Marble Palace. The garden contains no flower beds, but weaves together a progression of natural features such as flanking meadows, a stream, a rounded knoll and native deciduous trees. Although very natural and punctuated with stairways, paths, lovely gates, benches, bridges and a fountain, the garden is ordered and episodic. The garden won the Hunnewell Medal of the Massachusetts Horticultural Society, and the Garden Conservancy has recognized the garden as worthy of preservation.

Of the original 1,000 acres, most of the land was gifted to The Trustees for its protection. The farmhouse, studio and gardens were also given to the Trustees, and the studio, garden and woodland trails to the Marble Palace are open to public on a limited basis in the summer. The tours are self-guided, and reading material about the estate and its history is available in the studio for visitors who wish to learn more.

Garden at Ashintully - Courtesy of The Trustees

BERKSHIRE BOTANICAL GARDEN

5 West Stockbridge Road, Stockbridge, MA 01262
Website: www.berkshirebotanical.org
Phone: 413-298-3926
Season; May 1 through Columbus Day
Hours and Days of Operation: Daily: 9- 5PM
Garden Tours: 11 AM Monday through Sunday
Entry Fees: Adults $15 / Seniors $14 / Students $12 / Children under 12 Free

Berkshire Botanical Garden is located in Stockbridge about one-half mile from the center of town. Founded in 1934, local garden club members donated land as well as plants, love and knowledge of gardens and occasionally their gardeners. A visit to the Botanical Garden should be an educational and restful experience. Encompassing 15 acres, the garden begins at the top of a gradually sloping hill and then meanders along pathways through 27 different gardens to a pond at the bottom of the hill. Each of the 27 gardens has a different focus - lilies, primroses, herbs, etc.. The plants are well-marked and easily identified. Benches in the gardens allow visitors to rest, reflect and appreciate a very natural setting. More than 39 well-marked species of trees grow throughout the garden and provide shaded areas to sit.

Most of the gardens are located on the north side of Route 102, along with the Garden's recently renovated and refurbished Center House - a comfortable facility housing a botanical library, galleries, a teaching kitchen, classroom and office space. On the south side of Route 102, there is an educational center with a children's garden and vegetable garden as well as the visitor center where many of the plants on view in the garden are for sale. There is one daily guided tour at 11AM Monday through Saturday; otherwise, excellent maps of the gardens as well as many knowledgeable volunteers and staff will answer your questions and point you in the right direction. If you are a gardener, it is a great place to get ideas for your own garden.

Berkshire Botanical Garden

CONNECTICUT

The state of Connecticut is divided into two regions for touring purposes. The northern route begins in Woodstock and connects to Interstate 84 through Hartford and southwest to Woodbury and Bethlehem. The southern route is more coastal, and runs alongside I-95 from New London to Wilton.

<u>Northern Route</u>

With the exception of Hill-Stead and Roseland, most of the houses and gardens in this region date their origins to the era of the Revolutionary War and were the homes of individuals who were prominent in their individual communities, such as ministers (Glebe House and Bellamy-Faraday), or businessmen/lawyers who took advantage of the trade afforded by their regional rivers (Butler-McCook House and Webb-Deane-Stevens Museum). These houses are old, but over their lifetime, have undergone renovations and modernization (except Glebe House). Roseland was built in the 1850's and constructed as a summer retreat for a large family. It is one of the best examples of Gothic architecture in the United States, and it has an excellent example of a parterre garden. Hill-Stead was a "Gilded Age" house and like most of the houses in this region, it contains all the original contents of the house, including an exceptional collection of Impressionist art. Included in this region is the Elizabeth Park Rose Garden, which has no house but is famous for its rose garden with 15,000 bushes.

Southern Route

Beginning in New London, this route extends to Wilton, Connecticut near the New York border. The rest of the houses and gardens with the exception of Eolia were once part of working farms dating back to the 19th century. Weir Farm and the Griswold Museum evolved into gathering places for artists in the late 1800's, and Osborndale became a major breeder of dairy cows in the early 20th century. Located on Long Island Sound, Eolia is the only "Gilded Age" mansion on this coastal route and as part of a state park, offers opportunities for the beach and swimming.

INFORMATION REGARDING HOURS AND DAYS OF OPERATION AS WELL AS FEES AT EACH SITE ARE SUBJECT TO CHANGE AND IT IS BEST TO PHONE OR CHECK THE WEBSITE OF EACH LOCATION FOR UP-TO-DATE INFORMATION

Connecticut

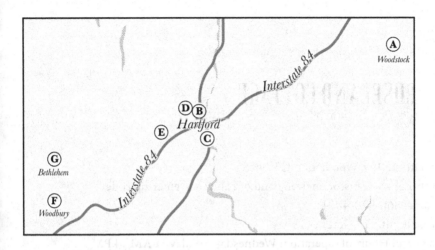

(A) Roseland Cottage
556 Route 169, Woodstock, CT

(B) Butler-McCook House
396 Main St, Hartford, CT

(C) Webb-Deane-Stevens Museum
211 Main St, Wethersfield, CT

(D) Elizabeth Park
1561 Asylum Ave, West Hartford, CT

(E) Hill-Stead Museum
35 Mountain Rd, Farmington, CT

(F) The Glebe House Museum +
Gertrude Jekyll Gardens
49 Hollow Rd, Woodbury, CT

(G) Bellamy-Ferriday House
9 Main St N, Bethlehem, CT

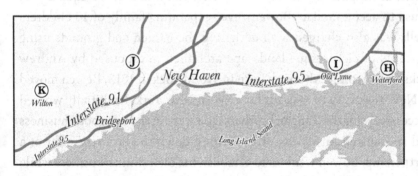

(H) Eolia
275 Great Neck Rd, Waterford, CT

(I) Florence Griswold Museum
96 Lyme St, Old Lyme, CT

(J) Osborne Homestead Museum
500 Hawthorne Ave, Derby, CT

(K) Weir Farm
735 Nod Hill Rd, Wilton, CT

ROSELAND COTTAGE

556 Route 169, Woodstock, CT 06281
Website: www.historicnewengland.org and then enter zip code
Phone: 860-928-4074
Season: June 1 - October 15
Days and Hours of Operation: Wednesday-Sunday 11 AM - 4 PM
House Tours: Tours on the hour with last tour at 4 PM
Entry Fees: $10 Adults / $9 Seniors / $5 students

Roseland Cottage is located in Woodstock, Connecticut - an old, beautiful and well-preserved New England town that lies between Providence, Rhode Island and Hartford, Connecticut. Roseland represents one of the best examples of Gothic Revival architecture in the country. In 1845, Henry Chandler Bowen (1813-1896) hired Joseph Wells, an English architect of churches, to build a 6,000 square foot house to accommodate Bowen's ever-expanding family of 10 children. Wells was also charged with designing the garden and grounds using concepts of picturesque landscape architecture espoused by Andrew Jackson Downing. Although born in Woodstock in 1813, Bowen moved to New York City to seek his fortune. In New York, he initially worked successfully for the Tappan brothers who were in the dry goods business and specialized in silk imports. Turning down the brothers' offer of a partnership, Bowen went on to establish his own similar business while marrying one of the brother's daughters, Lucy Tappan.

Henry and Lucy were committed to a life of virtue. As very religious members of the Congregational Church, they pursued a lifestyle in Woodstock which was free of sin (no smoking, dancing or alcohol) and allowed for an abundance of exercise and interaction with nature. They also were strong abolitionists, a political philosophy that led to Henry's active participation in the Republican party in the 1860's and the founding of "The Independent", a newspaper that espoused the virtues of temperance and the evils of slavery. His involvement with the Republicans led to visits to Roseland by many politicians including Grant, Harrison and Hayes. His politics also led to the bankruptcy of his main business prior to the Civil War, because Southerners refused to do business with him. Since he owned other businesses such as the newspaper, Henry survived the bankruptcy. In addition, Abraham Lincoln appointed him the tax collector in Brooklyn, New York, a profitable appointment as he was able to keep a percentage of the tax revenue. In 1863, Lucy died of complications of the birth of their tenth child. Henry married Ellen Holt two years later and had one additional child with her. He continued to summer in Woodstock with his 10 children and 14 grandchildren until his death in 1896. Until his death, the Bowens hosted a 4th of July celebration for the townsfolk that eventually became so big that he had to purchase a 60 acre property to accommodate the number of attendees. Ultimately, Henry left this property to the town to be used as a park.

Henry's second wife died in 1903, and Roseland was left to three of the ten children who continued to use the estate as a summer retreat. Between 1910 and 1920, the house was modernized with plumbing and electricity. The third generation took over the house in 1940 and until 1968, Henry's granddaughter lived there as a full-time resident. At her death, the family decided to sell the estate to Historic New England who purchased it given its historical and architectural significance. The sale included all of the family collections, archival material and furniture.

The house and its interior are unique. The exterior continues to be painted the same pink as it was in 1846. With its peaked windows, chimneys and its exaggerated vertical lines, the house is consistent with Gothic Revival architecture which seems to ascend upward to the heavens. The interior of the house is very rich with a wall covering called Lincrusta-Walton and a variety of Victorian and later-day furniture. The parterre garden is divided by two-foot boxwood hedges and planted each spring with 4,000 annuals. Maintaining the same garden design as the one in the 1840's, from Henry's bedroom and study, the garden resembles a Persian rug. Visitors can also explore the buildings on the property which include a barn, icehouse, woodhouse, the "his" and "hers" outdoor privy and the oldest bowling alley in the United States - the alley where President Grant celebrated his first strike by lighting up a cigar whereupon the owner told the President to step outside if he was going to smoke.

Roseland-Courtesy of Historic New England

BUTLER-MCCOOK HOUSE AND GARDEN

396 Main Street, Hartford, CT 06103
Website: www.ctlandmarks.org
Phone: 860-522-1806
Season: May through December
Days and Hours of Operation: May through September: Thursday through
    Sunday 12-4 PM; October through December: Saturday and Sunday
    12-4 PM
Entry Fees: $10 Adults / $8 Students and Seniors/ $5 Children (6-18)

The Butler-McCook House sits amid 10-story modern buildings on Main Street in Hartford, Connecticut. It is identifiable from a distance by an abundance of neighboring mature trees in sharp contrast to the glass and concrete of its neighbors. In its backyard is another historical house - the Amos Bull House.

The story of the house dates back to 1779 when Daniel Butler, the son of a tavern keeper, married Sarah Sheldon. Sarah's first husband had died in 1776 and left her with the responsibility of running his mills - a job she did very successfully. Daniel assumed the responsibility of running the mills, and the house was built in 1782. Their son, John Butler, inherited the house and mills in 1812, and his only child, Eliza Butler, at age 7, inherited the estate of her father, leaving her a rich woman. After her father's death, Eliza continued to live in the house with her mother and half-sister during the 1840's and 1850's. Taking advantage of her financial security, she traveled with her mother and half-sister to Europe, where she became fluent in French, studied art, painted and developed an interest in gardens. When she returned from Europe in 1865, she hired

Jacob Weidenmann to design a Victorian garden behind the house. It was around that time when she met John McCook.

John McCook, a cousin from Ohio, had served in the Civil War with his brothers and father. In 1862, he traveled to Hartford to attend Trinity College and boarded at Eliza's house. Apparently they got along, married in 1866 and had eight children. John became a minister and served as rector of St. John's Church in East Hartford from 1867 to 1927 without pay while teaching at Trinity College. He became very interested in what were then known as "tramps", now known as the "homeless", and he came to the conclusion that alcohol and lack of training, not lack of character and laziness, were critical factors in homelessness. Based on this, John recommended that victims of homelessness receive occupational training as well as therapeutic intervention for their alcoholism. He also suggested that an institution be built to carry out these goals. Lacking the necessary funding, his recommendations were never carried out.

John and Eliza's life was very full. Eliza continued to paint and the entire family was very musical. They spent their summers at a family house in Niantic, Connecticut (now a public park known as McCook Point). They traveled throughout the United States, Europe and Asia where their daughter was a missionary. They returned from each trip with mementos, and the house remains filled with unique objects from around the world.

Eliza died in 1917, and John in 1927. Four of the eight children never married and continued to live in the house until the last child died in 1971. The house, furnishings and collections were then turned over to Connecticut Landmarks for their perpetual preservation and as an educational tool to better understand Hartford history. The house has an education center in what once was a doctor's office for their son and not an original part of the house. The rest of the original part of the house tells the story of the family through paintings (Bierstadt), furniture, books, rose medallion china, antique toys and even Samurai armor - all collected since the house was built in 1782. Behind the house, there is a parterre garden with a central fountain, mature trees and gravel pathways. The garden extends one acre back to the Amos Bull House, and it continues to be well-maintained.

WEBB-DEANE-STEVENS MUSEUM

211 Main Street, Wethersfield, CT 06109
Website: www.webb-deane-stevens.org
Phone: 860-529-0612
Season: April through November
Days and Hour of Operation: May 1- October 31 daily except Tuesday 10 to 4
    PM and on Sunday 1-4 PM; In April and November Houses open Saturday
    10-4PM and Sunday 1-4 PM
Entry Fees: $12 Adults / $10 Seniors / $6 Students and Children (5-18)

The museum is comprised of three adjacent colonial houses that
stand on the main street of Wethersfield, Connecticut. Wethersfield
lies just south of Hartford and may be the oldest town in Connecticut.
Founded in 1634, the town prospered because of its proximity to the
Connecticut River, allowing it to participate in trade with the West Indies
by sending onions (valued for their content of Vitamin A and D and given
to slaves), tobacco, and metal goods in return for rum, molasses, tea and
coffee. Wealthy merchants, participating in the West Indian trade, often
built houses which broadcast their success.

Joseph Webb was one of these merchants, and in 1752, he completed
a three and half story house to accommodate his family of six children on
the first two floors. He used the top story and a half to house as many as
12 slaves and to act as warehouse. Joseph died in 1761, leaving the house
to his 12 year old son, Joseph, Jr., and leaving his widow, Mehitable, to care
for the children as well as to run the shipping business. Overwhelmed,
Mehitable turned to Silas Deane.

Silas (1737-1789), the son of a blacksmith from Groton, Connecticut,

— 161 —

attended Yale on a scholarship, sat for the Bar, and eventually ended up in Wethersfield to practice law. At age 24, he started to help Webb's widow and two years later, married her in 1763. Together, they had one son and in 1767, Mehitable died of tuberculosis. In 1769, Silas remarried another rich widow who was politically connected in Connecticut. About this time the Deane house was completed for his new wife and his only son, Jesse. This house was next to the Webb house, thereby allowing Silas to keep an eye on his six step-children as well as his trading business. The new house not only demonstrated Silas's success, but it also served as a place to entertain influential people who might help him achieve his political aspirations. Consequently, he served in Connecticut's Colonial Assembly, Connecticut's Committee of Correspondence, and the First Continental Congress in Philadelphia. In 1775, Silas helped plan and finance the capture of Fort Ticonderoga, and eventually, he was sent to Paris in 1776 to help Benjamin Franklin and Arthur Lee negotiate the sale of arms and supplies from the French. Franklin and Silas got along well, but Lee accused both of them of embezzling money used for the purchase of these supplies. Although Franklin was able to clear his name, Silas was not. Discouraged by the progress of the war and his rejection by his countrymen, he wrote letters to family members questioning the wisdom of the Revolution. These letters were publicized and he was accused of treason. By 1789, his second wife had died, and he was bankrupt. Like Joseph Webb Jr., he had lent the Revolutionary government money for which he was never reimbursed. In 1789, he mysteriously died, possibly by poison administered by his assistant.

Because of the bankruptcies of their owners, the Webb and Deane houses and their furnishings were sold in 1790. However, the interiors were maintained and preserved by subsequent owners who appreciated the historic value of the houses.

The third house of the museum, the Stevens House, was the last of the three to be built. Built in 1789 by a leatherworker, Isaac Stevens, it is neither as large nor grand as the other two houses. Its importance lies in the fact that the Stevens family continued to live there for 170 years. As a result, the contents of the first floor are all original, and the manufactured wallpaper and carpets reflect the influence of the Industrial Age. All three contiguous houses now belong to the Colonial Dames of Connecticut who have restored them to their appropriate periods. As earlier noted, the contents of the Stevens House are original on the first floor, but the second floor contains a toy collection. Although the Deane house contents are not original, documents have enabled the Colonial Dames to refurnish the house with appropriate period antiques and furnishings. The same is true of the Webb house, except the walls of the first floor are decorated with Colonial murals painted under the direction of Wallace Nutting. Guided tours of the houses are available every day except Tuesdays.

Behind the three houses is a common five-acre lot centered by a barn. The lot is mowed and has an apple orchard. In 1921, the Colonial Dames hired Amy Cogswell to design a garden behind the middle house (Webb house). It is a Colonial Revival garden with arbors and pathways, and unlike most colonial gardens, is more decorative than functional.

Webb House at the Webb-Deane-Stevens Museum

ELIZABETH PARK

1561 Asylum Avenue, West Hartford, CT 06117
Website: http://elizabethparkct.org
Phone: 860-231-9443
Season: Open all year
Hours of Operation: Dawn To dusk
Tours of the Garden: Available in the summer-check website
Entry fees: Free

Elizabeth Park, located in both West Hartford (82 acres) and Hartford (19 acres), Connecticut, was a gift to the city of Hartford by Charles H. Pond in honor of his wife Elizabeth. Mr. Pond was a wealthy businessman and politician who inherited the property as a farm from his father, and as early as 1870 consulted with Olmsted about the possibility of transforming the farm into a city park. Predeceased by his wife and childless, he left the land plus an endowment of $100,000 to the City of Hartford to be used for the construction of a city park. In 1896, the city of Hartford hired Swiss-born landscape architect, Theodore Wirth, to design the park. Working with Olmsted's firm, the final design of the park reflects a combination of two schools of landscape design: the European formal gardens of Wirth and the natural settings of Olmsted with serpentine roadways, sweeping vistas, ponds and bridges.

The park is most famous for its rose garden. Designed by Wirth in 1904, it is our country's oldest public rose garden. Originally one acre in size and 132 rose beds, the rose garden was later extended to 2.5 acres and 475 beds with 15,000 rose bushes and 800 varieties of roses. As the 3rd largest rose garden in the United States, it is a major draw to the park, especially in June and early July when it is at its peak. A sequence of archways covered by roses runs down the middle of the rose garden and meets in a central gazebo enveloped by Virginia Creepers.

Next to the rose garden is a perennial garden, and below that are rock and shade gardens which are well marked and recently restored. Between the greenhouses and the perennial garden, a tulip garden is planted in the spring with 11,000 tulip bulbs, which are later dug up to make room for the annual garden. The park also has a restaurant and snackbar which borders one of the ponds and is surrounded by garden paths.

HILL-STEAD MUSEUM

35 Mountain Road, Farmington, CT 06032
Website: www.hillstead.org
Phone:860-677-4787
Season: Year round
Hours and Days of Operation; Required guided tours of the museum Tuesday-
    Sunday 10-4 PM - Last tour at 3 PM
Entry Fees: $15 adults / $12 seniors and students / $8 children 6-12 / Free
    children under 6

Located in Farmington, Connecticut on a hill overlooking rolling
pastures and the Litchfield hills, Hill-Stead, built in 1901, was a grand
yet comfortable home for 45 years. Today the estate is a museum that
houses a remarkable collection of art and preserves the work of the first
American female architect. This house-museum and garden are the result
of a collaborative effort between a father, Alfred Pope (1842-1913), a
mother, Ada Brooks Pope (1844-1920), and their headstrong daughter,
Theodate (1867-1946).

Born in Maine, Alfred moved to Ohio where he eventually worked at
the Cleveland Malleable Iron Company, and at the age of 37, he became
its president in 1879. This company produced an exceptionally strong
form of iron which was critical for the production of rails and other
railroad products. The success of the company made Alfred Pope a very
wealthy man and allowed him to collect remarkable works of art. Unlike
other "Gilded Age" collectors, Pope collected contemporary art (at that
time - Impressionism) rather than the "old masters". He also used his own
judgement and tastes to dictate his choice of art rather than relying on an

advisor to make choices for him. The result is a collection that not only includes the Impressionists (Cassatt, Degas, Manet, Monet and Whistler), but also includes mainstream artists (Pierre Puvis de Chavannes and Eugene Carriere) as well as Asian, American and European prints.

Alfred and Ada had one child, a daughter christened Effie, who was described as headstrong and set on charting the path of her own life rather than following the expected and prescribed course. She was sent to all the best schools in Cleveland and completed her education at Miss Porter's School in Farmington, where she was to be polished and prepared to move into her role in society. At that time in her life she made two decisions: 1) to take the name of her paternal grandmother Theodate (meaning "Gift of God") and 2) to live in New England in a rural setting. After a 10-month grand tour throughout Europe and a debutante season in Cleveland, she moved back to Farmington and bought and renovated an old 18th century farmhouse. Theodate happily lived on her own for nearly 10 years before convincing her parents to join her in Farmington.

Alfred bought 250 acres of rolling farmland near Theodate's house and engaged McKim, Mead, and White to design what was to become a 33,000-square foot Colonial Revival house with a working farm, gardens and a small 6 hole golf course. Although this firm was hired to do the design, Theodate designed the house and got technical support from the firm. Although her architectural training was limited to a few courses, the house was acclaimed by the architectural community. In June 1901, the Popes moved from Cleveland to Farmington with their art collection and spent the rest of their years at Hill-Stead until Albert's death in 1913 and Ada's in 1920.

The architectural success of Hill-Stead launched Theodate's career. Subsequently, she designed Westover School in Middlebury, Connecticut and then Avon Old Farms School in Avon, Connecticut with a handful of other schools and private residences in between. Avon Old Farms was to be a progressive boy's school and was financed, designed and constructed by Theodate. The school's architecture was Old World with its roots in the Cotswolds region of England. The school opened in 1927 but construction continued into the late 1930's. The original plan, consisting of a second quadrangle, was never completed, possibly for financial reasons, as occasionally Theodate would selectively have to sell off one of her father's paintings to cover construction costs. During World War II, the school was used as a rehabilitation hospital for soldiers, but eventually reopened after the war.

Theodate moved into Hill-Stead shortly after her 1916 marriage to career diplomat, John Wallace Riddle. It was a first marriage for both. Theodate was 49 and John was 51. As a single woman in 1914, Theodate took in the first of three foster sons. The first child, Gordon, died of polio at age three. The other two boys, Paul and Donald, joined the household in 1917 and 1918. None of the boys were ever officially adopted, but rather raised as wards. Paul and Donald were educated in the best schools, and Donald recalled fond memories of growing up with Aunt Theo and Uncle John. Theodate died in 1946, leaving instructions in her will that Hill-Stead should be open to the public, maintained as a museum and that its art collection and architecture never changed. Following Theodate's instructions, the house and gardens, furnishings and collections are well maintained and remain as they were in 1946.

Originally designed by Theodate but updated in 1920 by Beatrix Farrand, the sunken garden can be seen from the house on the hill. Enclosed by a 10 foot stone wall, octagonal shaped yew hedges surround the Colonial Revival garden which is centered by a shaded, elongated summer house and lawn. The design of the garden gives the visitor a sense of complete privacy. The grounds outside the garden allow views of rolling hills, the pond and stone walls. While at Hill-Stead, visitors may wish to explore three miles of hiking trails that lead through woodlands, swamps, around a pond and into the fields. The house tours are guided, and particular attention is given to Alfred Pope's collection of art that hangs throughout house. The furnishings are all original to the house.

Hill-stead

THE GLEBE HOUSE MUSEUM & GERTRUDE JEKYLL GARDEN

49 Hollow Road, Woodbury, CT 06798
Website: www.glebehousemuseum.org
Phone: 203-263-2855
Season: May-October
Hours and days of operation: Wednesday-Sunday 1-4 PM (Garden is open
    dawn to dusk).
Entry Fees: $7 adult/$2 child under

Glebe House is not named for its first owner, but is a word defined as
"a piece of land serving as part of a clergyman's benefice and providing
income". For John Rutgers Marshall (1743-1789), the house was also
part of his glebe. The house was built around 1750 and was grander than
most at that time with three stories rather than two. Architecturally, the
house was unusual in that it was a combination of gambrel and salt box
styles. In 1771, a group of citizens belonging to the Anglican church of
Woodbury, Connecticut asked John Marshall to move from New York
to serve as the first Anglican minister of Woodbury - one of the largest
towns in Connecticut at that time. They offered the house and seven
acres for John to farm as a glebe.

John arrived with two small children, his wife Sarah and two slaves.
Presumably, he thrived in his new position as he added seven more
children over the ensuing years. His good fortune turned as the American
Revolution progressed, since he became suspect as a traitor or loyalist to
the king due to his association with the Anglican church. It is not clear

whether John was a loyalist, but apparently he was pulled out of a church service and stoned by the Committee of Inspection. John died in 1789 and may have died of complications from this stoning.

In 1783, a secret election was held in the election room of Glebe House, nominating Samuel Seabury to be the first American bishop of the Episcopal Anglican Church. Before that, it was required that the ordination of an Episcopal minister occur only in England by a bishop, since there were none in the colonies. This process was expensive, time consuming and dangerous because it required crossing the Atlantic to receive this ordination. After his election, Seabury sailed to England to be consecrated as bishop, but when he refused to pledge allegiance to the king, he had to go to Scotland to receive this consecration. As a result, the Scottish Book of Prayer was used in the American church.

After the Marshalls left Glebe House, it was occupied by Gideon Boxford and his family until 1866. Gideon, apparently, was a silversmith and had no relationship with the church. Subsequently, the house may have been used as a retirement home for clergy and as a boarding house. The house gradually deteriorated and was at risk of demolition, when in 1892, three gentleman, recognizing the house's historical significance in the founding of the Episcopal Church in America, purchased the house for $300 and gave it as a Christmas present to Bishop John Williams. In 1922, The Seabury Society for the Preservation of Glebe House was formed, and the house was restored to be used as a museum in 1925.

The house is open to the public for guided tours. Although most of the furniture is not original to the house, many of the pieces are of Woodbury provenance, include a few Marshall family pieces and are appropriate to the period. There are also many household implements whose uses are well-described by the guides.

The garden is open from dawn until dusk and was completed in the 1990's, despite having been designed in 1926. At the time of the house restoration, Anna Burr Jennings, an heiress to the Standard Oil fortune, commissioned an English garden designer, Gertrude Jekyll, to design an old-fashioned New England garden. Gertrude, then 86 years old, was famous for her designs of English gardens, having designed over 350 in her career. However, she never visited Glebe House and its grounds, and admitted that she was unfamiliar with plants which would grow in the Connecticut climate. Despite this, she submitted plans for the garden and for reasons that are unclear, they were never implemented. In the late 1970's, the plans resurfaced in the papers of Beatrix Farrand at the University of California at Berkeley and were used by volunteers to create today's garden. It is the only surviving garden of Gertrude Jekyll in the United States.

Glebe House

BELLAMY-FERRIDAY HOUSE AND GARDEN

9 Main Street North, Bethlehem, CT 06751
Website: www.ctlandmarks.org
Phone: 203-266-7596
Season: May through October
Day and Hours of Operation: May through September:Friday through Monday
    12 to 4 PM; October: Saturday and Sunday 12 to 4 PM
Entry Fees: $10 Adult / $8 Seniors and Students/ $5 Children (6-18) / Children
    under 6 Free

Bethlehem, Connecticut, sitting between Woodbury and
Torrington, is the location of the Bellamy-Ferriday House. In the
countryside surrounded by stately trees, the house looks down on the
property once owned by Reverend Joseph Bellamy. Joseph was born
in 1719 to a farming family, and was clearly a prodigy. He enrolled as
Yale at age 12 and graduated four years later as a minister. His mentor,
after graduation, was Jonathan Edwards, and together they espoused
the religious belief that God was more forgiving than the God of the
Anglican and Congregational Church. This new belief allowed for more
freedom of thought and became a challenge to the overbearing authority
of the governor or king. This was called the "First Great Awakening", and
this new way of thinking was thought to be one of the seeds that led to
the American Revolution. In 1738, the 15 families of Bethlehem asked
Bellamy to found a church, because the distance to Woodbury was too
far to travel every Sunday. In return, the congregation gave him a house
and 100 acres to farm. At age 71, Joseph died a wealthy man, leaving
550 acres of farmland, a library and the farmhouse (enlarged from his

original house since Joseph ran a theology school with a dormitory at the farmhouse graduating over 60 students).

Descendants of Joseph continued to farm the property until 1868, when it passed out of the family and was bought by the Hull Family to be used as a summer retreat. The exterior of the house at that time was reconfigured to be more Victorian with the addition of a porte cochere, porches and bay windows. From 1868 to 1902, the house and property slowly declined until Eliza and Henry Ferriday bought the property. Caroline, their only child, was sickly and convinced her parents that they should purchase the property despite their very strong misgivings. The Ferridays were rich Manhattan socialites who had the means to restore the house and garden to reflect the spirit of Joseph Bellamy since their daughter Caroline was obsessed with his legacy. Edson Gage, a Colonial Revival specialist, was hired to create this transformation, and Caroline and her mother spent the rest of their lives filling the house with furniture, books and paintings that Bellamy might have had.

Because of her health, Caroline was tutored at home, but in her early 20's, she became an actress on Broadway. Always a student and traveler, Caroline became a great admirer of Napoleon and Charles de Gaulle. During World War II, she volunteered at the French consulate, and at the end of the war, she met de Gaulle's niece, who had escaped from a German concentration camp called Ravenbrook. She told Caroline about the medical experimentation done on women prisoners, particularly Poles. Caroline spent the next 15 years locating as many of these women as possible and bringing them to the United States for medical care. Initially, Caroline and others were underwriting the cost of this effort. Because of her determination to publicize this injustice, eventually she and Norman Cousins involved the U.S. Senate who put pressure on the German government to compensate these women in the 1960's. This story is documented in a book called "Lilac Girls".

Caroline never married. Her mother died in 1954, and Caroline died in 1990. In her later years, she continued on with her philanthropic efforts. She was very involved in land conservation and funded the Bethlehem Land Trust. She gave 80 acres of her land to the trust and kept 10 acres with the house. Having no heirs and wanting to perpetuate

Joseph Bellamy's legacy, she gave the house, its contents and 10 acres to Connecticut Landmarks.

The house is open for guided tours several days a week. For the most part, the furnishings are not original to Bellamy's time but represent what Caroline and her mother felt were appropriate for that time and Bellamy's spirit. The garden was created in the 1920's and terraced since the house was located on a hill. The upper part is a parterre garden based on the design of an oriental rug, symmetrical and edged with yew hedges. As one descends down the terraces, the gardens open up with the last level being an orchard.

Side view of Bellamy-Ferriday House

▪ EOLIA

275 Great Neck Road, Waterford, CT 06385
Website: www.ct.gov/deep/cwp/view.asp
Phone 860-443-5725
Season: Park-Year round; Mansion-Memorial Day Weekend to Labor Day
   Weekend
Days and Hours of Operation: Park - 8 AM to sunset; Mansion Tours-Saturday,
   Sundays and holidays Memorial Day to Labor Day - 10 AM to 2 PM
Entry Fees: Parking lot fee on weekends only

Eolia is the name of the 42-room summer retreat in Waterford, Connecticut just west of New London. Located on a 230-acre farm on Long Island Sound, its name is derived from Aeolus, the Greek god of wind. Originally built by Mrs. Harkness's sister in 1906 in the Roman Renaissance Revival style, Mr. and Mrs. Edward Harkness purchased the house in 1907. At that time, Mr. Harkness employed the services of his friend and Yale classmate - John Gamble Rogers - to convert the interior of the mansion to a Neo-Classical style, redesign the gardens and add the carriage house which is as large as the main house. Eolia was one of the seven residences owned by Harkness.

Edward Harkness was the son of an Ohio harness maker, brewer and then banker who had the good fortune of being an original investor in John D. Rockefeller's Standard Oil. Edward attended St. Paul's, Yale and Columbia Law School. Although well-prepared to enter the world of commerce, he decided to enter the world of philanthropy because in 1916, he had inherited a large fortune left at the death of his parents and older brother. At his brother's death, Edward was the third-largest stockholder in Standard Oil. In 1918, he was Forbes Magazine's sixth-richest man in the United States. His philanthropic interests covered a broad range of activities including hospitals (Columbia Presbyterian Hospital), the Metropolitan Museum of Art in New York and other educational pursuits. In the late 1920's, he became interested in introducing the English system of residential colleges to the United States as a means of enhancing educational exchange by redistributing and focusing the student population into smaller units. Originally, he offered to build such a system for his alma mater, Yale, but his offer was rejected. He then made the same proposal to Harvard who accepted, and with $10 million was able to complete the "house system" (8 small colleges within the larger college) in 1931. This gift essentially provided Harvard a way of organizing residential life for all classes except the freshman. Yale, seeing their mistake, then reconsidered Harkness's proposal and accepted $11 million to build nine residential colleges.

Mr. Harkness died in 1940 at the age of 66, and his wife died 10 years later. Having no children, they left Eolia with its 230 acres to the state of Connecticut, which now runs it as a state park. The park is open from sunrise to dusk and includes open fields, picnic areas and beach facilities. Located in a separate area of the park, the mansion is well-maintained but only open to the public on weekends from 10 AM to 2 PM from Memorial Day to Labor Day. However, one can get a good sense of the beauty of the mansion by looking through the windows on the first floor. The house is a popular wedding venue and is generally unfurnished on the first floor. The carriage house is not open to the public, but is worth visiting to look through the windows at the paneled, dusty billiard room of Harkness's time. On the weekends, a gift shop is open in one part of the carriage house. Located behind the house with views onto Long Island Sound, the main gardens are exquisite. Initially designed by Harkness's architect friend, John Rogers, they were further refined by Beatrix Farrand from 1918 to 1924. The garden to the west is Italianate and ends at a gate which leads down through a boxwood garden and eventually to a rock garden with a small pool. To the east of the house is another garden that is less enclosed, revealing views of Long Island Sound and Fisher's Island. Finally, a cutting garden sits between the main house and the carriage house.

Eolia

FLORENCE GRISWOLD MUSEUM

96 Lyme Street, Old Lyme, CT 06371
Website: florencegriswoldmuseum.org
Phone: 860-434-5542
Season: All year
Hours and Days of Operation: Tuesday-Saturday 10-5 PM, Sunday 1-5 PM
Entry Fees: $10 adults, $9 seniors, $8 students, children free 12 and under

Along the banks of the Lieutenant River which eventually runs into the Connecticut River sits the Florence Griswold Museum. The museum occupies a Georgian house built in 1817, and is the home for a private collection of American Impressionist art created from the early 1900's to the 1930's by Florence Griswold (1850-1937).

Florence was not a painter nor was she a rich woman - rather, she was a spinster who ran a boarding house in Old Lyme, Connecticut. Her story really begins with her father when in the 1840's, Captain Robert Griswold purchased the Georgian mansion as a home for his wife and four children for $3,000. Captain Griswold was a successful sea captain who ran packing ships between New York and London, and this success allowed him to buy the house. In the 1860's, he decided to retire but then lost his money on a bad investment in a nail company. To survive, the family ran a finishing school for young women in the house, and when that failed, a boarding house. After inheriting the house, Florence continued to run the house as a boarding house, taking advantage of the increasing demand in the late 1890's by city folk to escape the evils of urbanization brought by the Industrial Revolution.

One of her boarders was Henry Ward Ranger - an artist of the

"Tonalist" school who was seeking to start an artists' colony where artists could congregate, work together and share ideas. Old Lyme was the perfect location because of its accessibility to New York by train and its rural environment that harkened back to simpler times. Together, Florence (then age 50, hospitable and motherly) and Mr. Ranger attracted mature artists to come for the summer to paint and to have a good time. For $7 a week, an artist received room and board and the use of a privy in the backyard. Couples got the use of the bedrooms, but the rest of the artists slept in a bunk room in the attic with an occupancy of 17. Florence ran this operation from 1900-1934. Her most famous visiting artist was Ellen WIlson and her husband Woodrow (before his presidency).

These artists became Florence's family and for the artists, this retreat was a second home. In 1910, Florence ran into some financial difficulties after modernizing the house with one bathroom, electricity and a telephone. While Florence was away during the winter, the artists without her knowledge, returned to Lyme, painted and wallpapered the house and also purchased new rugs and furniture. There was also a tradition of the artists painting scenes on the panels of doors and the dining room. Over the years, other paintings done by the boarders were given to Florence. Most of these were done by American Impressionist artists despite the fact that Florence's co-founder was a "Tonalist".

In 1934, Florence was forced to sell the boarding house because of debts. Despite the efforts of the artists to buy it, it was bought by someone outside the colony who built a house right next to the river. Florence was allowed to stay in the old boarding house until her death in 1937, at which point the contents of the house with the exception of the paintings, were sold off. In 1941, the Old Lyme Historical Society purchased the house and opened it as a museum in 1947.

The house is open all year round. The second floor of the house is a gallery hung with works mostly by American Impressionist painters (Childe Hassam, Willard Metcalf) and also Tonalist paintings (Henry Ward Ranger, William Henry Howe). In addition to the painted panels in the dining room and on the doors, the first floor has many works of art given to Florence by her boarders. The first floor has been restored to recreate the boarding house as it was in its heyday. Outside, the gardens extend behind the house and are a combination of vegetables and flowers in accordance with plans dating back to Florence's father. Beyond the garden is a long lawn which slowly drops down to the river with a view of the marshes beyond. Shading the lawn are trees that are at least 100 years old. A new gallery/museum was built near the river about 10 years ago that accommodates exhibitions that change quarterly. It is well situated so as to not affect one's view of the river and marshes. Visitors may enjoy lunch outdoors at the restaurant overlooking the river.

Florence Griswold Museum

OSBORNE HOMESTEAD MUSEUM

500 Hawthorne Avenue, Derby, CT 06418
Website: www.ct.gov/deep/kellogg
Phone: 203-734-2513
Season: May - December
Hours and Days of Operation: Thursday and Friday 10-3 PM; Saturday 10-
    4PM and Sunday 12 -4 PM
Days of House Tours: Thursday-Sunday
Entry Fees: Free

Located northwest of New Haven, the Osborne Homestead Museum is located in Derby - the smallest city in the state of Connecticut. For many centuries, Native Americans known as the Paugussetts inhabited this region. The colonial history of Derby dates back to the 1630's, when Dutch fur traders were drawn to the area for its abundance of beavers and its location, which allowed easy transport of the pelts down the Housatonic River to Long Island Sound. When the beaver population was depleted, commerce turned to agriculture and manufacturing. As a means of transport, the river continued to be an important factor in Derby's development since the city is only 13 miles north of the Atlantic.

Today, the museum encompasses a farmhouse, gardens, an environmental center and over 418 acres of fields, woodland trails, ponds and a passageway down to the Housatonic. The house and land were a gift to the state of Connecticut in the 1950's by Frances (Fanny) Eliza Osborne Kellogg (1876-1956). Frances was the granddaughter of John W. Osborne, one of the Naugatuck Valley early industrial entrepreneurs. In 1870, he bought the farmhouse at 500 Hawthorne Avenue for his newlywed son, Wilbur. After serving in the Civil War as a gunnery officer, Frances' father, Major Wilbur Osborne, took over his father's business, Osborne and Cheeseman Company and several other manufacturing companies in Derby. The products of his company ranged from islets for shoes and corsets, the hoops for corsets, sheet metal and silver plating.

Major Osborne was also interested in agriculture, and during his lifetime Osborne imported livestock to start a dairy and trotting horse farm at Osbornedale. At his death in 1907, he left the farm and his business holdings to his only surviving child, Frances. The expectation was that Frances would sell the business. However, she had worked as her father's assistant from an early age and was fully prepared to take over the companies. She accomplished this successfully, and over the ensuing years, she increased the size and number of companies.

At age 43, she married Waldo Kellogg (1870-1928). Waldo had grown up in Kansas, but was sent east to study architecture at Cornell. Subsequently, he worked as an architect in New York at McKim, Mead, and White as well as at Carrier and Hastings. Later, as an architect in New Haven, he designed the Allington Veteran's Hospital. At some point, Fanny's and Waldo's paths crossed leading to marriage in 1919. They lived at Osbornedale, but never had children. Soon after their marriage, they remodeled the original farmhouse in the Colonial Revival style and added a wing to accommodate Waldo's office and studio.

Taking an active interest in animal husbandry, they started breeding Holstein-Friesian cattle - a breed brought from the Netherlands around 1621. At its peak, the farm had 141 cows - 40 for milking and the rest for breeding. The farm's cows were considered very valuable because of their high productivity. For instance, one cow was a record holder who produced 30,000 pounds of milk in one year (normal is 6,000 pounds). The daughter of this record holder was sold for $1.2 million. The bull - named Osbornedale Ivanhoe - was also sought after and sired over 11,000 production tested daughters and 5,500 classified daughters. With the advent of artificial insemination, Ivanhoe was highly sought after, and his semen was worth more than $10,000 a vial.

Waldo died in 1928, and Frances continued to live a very active life - running the businesses, the dairy and contributing in significant ways to civic affairs in Derby. In the early 1950's, during a housing shortage in the United States, a federal program threatened to take portions of Osbornedale by imminent domain for affordable housing. With hours to spare, Frances saved the property by giving it to the state of Connecticut to be used as a park and museum after her death and the death of her housekeeper. Frances died in 1956, but her housekeeper lived at the house until 1976 when she died at 101.

The house, gardens and environmental center with its trails and educational programs are open Thursday through Sunday from May to October. Tours of the house are guided and the contents of the house original to at least Frances's time. Off the sun porch, there is a formal garden which is an extension of the porch. The garden is terraced, sunken and has symmetrical pathways of brick that define the squared-off beds. Through an arbor is a sundial garden. A rock garden and a butterfly garden lie beyond the formal garden, and there are remnants of an orchard near the house. Within walking distance of the house, the environmental center has exhibits which focus on Derby, the rivers, the Osborne family and finally the habitat of the farm.

Osborne Homestead Museum

WEIR FARM NATIONAL HISTORIC SITE

735 Nod Hill Road, Wilton, CT 06897
Website:www.nps.gov/wefa
Phone: 203-834-1896
Season: May 1-October 31
Hours and Days of Operation: Wednesday through Sunday, 10-4 PM
Entry Fees: Free

Julian Alden Weir (1852-1919) was the 14th child of Robert Walter Weir, a well-respected Hudson River School artist and professor of drawing at West Point. Like his father and brother (John Ferguson Weir - the first dean of the Yale School of Fine Arts), Julian demonstrated great talent as a boy and studied at the National Academy of Design. From 1873 to 1877, he was able to study in Paris at the Ecole des Beaux Arts due to the generosity of his godfather's widow (Mrs. Alden), a gift that caused him to sign all his future paintings "J. Alden" rather than "Julian". While in Europe, he received a very classical and realistic approach to painting, and on seeing his first exhibition of Impressionist art, he was very disdainful.

In 1877, Weir returned to New York and established himself as a portrait painter as well as an art teacher. In 1882, he fell in love with Anna Baker, a student in his class, and they quickly became engaged. That same year, Julian agreed to trade a painting that he had bought in New York for a 153-acre farm in Branchville, Connecticut, an hour train ride from the City. It was in Branchville that Julian's art became less realistic and more in keeping with the evolving Impressionism of the late 19th Century. His marriage to Anna also took some financial pressure off of

Weir and allowed him more freedom to experiment artistically as Anna was from a wealthy family. Julian and Anna had four children: Julian Jr., who died at age 1, Caroline, Dorothy and Cora. Sadly, in 1892, Anna died of complications of childbirth one week after Cora was born, and Julian asked his sister-in-law Ella, to take charge of the children while he recovered from his loss of Anna by working at the World's Columbia Exposition in Chicago with Sanford White.

The following year he and Ella married and expanded the farm by purchasing an adjoining farm (the Webb Farm) bringing the total acreage to 238 acres. In addition, he built a pond and continued to maintain crops and livestock, insisting that farm equipment be driven by oxen and horses rather than more modern mechanical equipment. He believed that the use of animals made the farm more aesthetically pleasing to paint. During his years with Ella, he entertained many other artists at the farm including Childe Hassam, John Twachtman and John Singer Sargent - all of whom would stay and paint with him. In 1919, Julian died as a leader of the American Impressionist style which was more realistic than French Impressionism.

After Julian's death, Dorothy, the second daughter and a gifted artist, moved into the main farmhouse and took care of the farm and her step-mother until 1931 when Ella died. In 1932, Dorothy married Mahonri Mackintosh Young, a sculptor, painter and grandson of Brigham Young (a founder of the Mormon Church). Much of Dorothy's time was occupied by documenting and perpetuating her father's legacy which ultimately led to the publication of a book *"The Life and Letters of J. Alden Weir"*. Dorothy died in 1946 and Mahonri in 1957. After Mahonri's death, his two children from a previous marriage sold a portion of the farm to Sperry and Doris Andrews, who were artists, friends of their father and interested in protecting the farm's legacy and open space. It was primarily Doris's persistence and energy that led to the acquisition of Weir Farm by the National Park Service.

Cora Weir Burlingham, Weir's youngest daughter, was given the adjoining property (Webb Farm) at her father's death. Cora had studied landscape design, botany and horticulture. She both worked at and served on the board of the New York Botanical Garden. On inheriting Webb farm, Cora commissioned local landscape architect Vera Poggi Green to design a sunken garden behind the farmhouse. Cora also added terraced gardens to the south and restored the "secret garden" to the north. She was also instrumental in helping her sister Dorothy's efforts to document her father's life and to protect the land from development by establishing the 110-acre Weir Preserve adjacent to the park.

The farm, studios, houses and 60 acres of the original 238 acres are now open to the public under the auspices of the National Park Service. While the grounds are open from dawn to dusk 12 months a year, the two houses and two artist's studios are open from May 1st - Oct 31st. Preceded by a 15 minute video, visits to the houses and studios are guided and take about one hour. The contents of the house and studios are largely original, although some of Weir's paintings are not, since many reside in private collections and museums. Unlike the richness of its interiors, the exterior of the farmhouse is simple. The sunken garden is unique and was featured in the 1956 publication of *The Treasury of American Gardens*. Walking trails lead to the pond and around the grounds. The extensive stone walls, many of which were designed by Cora, are impressive.

Sunken Garden at Weir Farm

HUDSON VALLEY
AND VICINITIES

From the Bronx to Albany, New York and along the eastern edge of the Hudson River is a series of gardens and estates associated with historic houses. The exceptions are Untermeyer Park, Stonecrop, Blithewood and Innisfree, where the garden and grounds have been maintained, but the houses are no longer available for touring, as they either have been torn down or used for another function. Not all of the sites in this section are on the Hudson, but lie east of the Hudson River estates and are close to the others (Weathersfield and Innisfree).

The development of the Hudson Valley took place in two stages. From Albany southwards, the first stage began before the Revolutionary War and was controlled by the Livingston family who owned thousands of acres along the Hudson down to Hyde Park. On this riverfront property, they built large estates with farmland and woodlands for timbering and used the river to transport their products. By the mid-19th century, these estates were transformed from places of commerce to those of escape and relaxation. With the invention of the steamboat in the early 1800's and construction of the railroads, owners could live in New York and escape to their estates on the weekends and during the summer.

The estates from New York City north were built later, and their construction resulted from the rapid growth of Manhattan with its subsequent deplorable sanitary conditions and the improved accessibility provided by the development of the steamboat and the railroads. These estates were mostly built from the 1830's to the early 20th century, and they provided the rich with a means of escaping the congestion of a rapidly expanding New York City. The scale of the houses, gardens and landscapes is generally grander than those further north and were meant to communicate the financial success of their owners. Large staffs were required to maintain them, and by the mid 20th century, it became impractical to maintain them. Thus, they have become house museums open to the public.

INFORMATION REGARDING HOURS AND DAYS OF OPERATION AS WELL AS FEES AT EACH SITE ARE SUBJECT TO CHANGE AND IT IS BEST TO PHONE OR CHECK THE WEBSITE OF EACH LOCATION FOR UP-TO -DATE INFORMATION

Hudson Valley & Vicinity

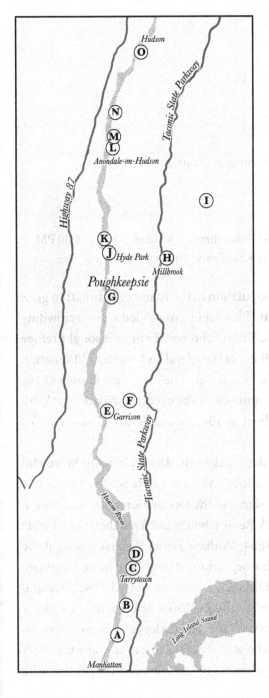

(A) Wave Hill
649 W 249th St, Bronx, NY

(B) Untermeyer Park & Gardens
945 N Broadway, Yonkers, NY

(C) Lyndhurst
635 S Broadway, Tarrytown, NY

(D) Kykuit
381 N Broadway, Sleepy Hollow, NY

(E) Boscobel House & Gardens
1601 NY-9D, Garrison, NY

(F) Stonecrop Gardens
81 Stonecrop Ln, Cold Spring, NY

(G) Locust Grove
2683 South Rd, Poughkeepsie, NY

(H) Innisfree Garden
362 Tyrrel Rd, Millbrook, NY

(I) Wethersfield
88 Wethersfield Way, Amenia, NY

(J) Home of Franklin D. Roosevelt
National Historic Site
*4097 Albany Post Rd,
Hyde Park, NY*

(K) Vanderbilt Mansion
National Historic Site
*119 Vanderbilt Park Rd,
Hyde Park, NY*

(L) Montgomery Place
*55 Gardener Way,
Annandale-on-the-Hudson, NY*

(M) Blithewood
75 Blithewood Ave, Red Hook, NY

(N) Clermont
1 Clermont Ave, Germantown, NY

(O) Olana
5720 State Route 9G, Hudson, NY

WAVE HILL

West 249th Street+Independence Avenue, Bronx, NY 10471
Website: www.wavehill.org
Phone: 718-549-3200
Season: Year Round
Days and Hours of Operation: Tuesday through Sunday- 9 AM to 4:30 PM
Entry Fees: $8 Adult/ $4 Seniors + Students/ Parking - $8

From 1800 to 1830, the population of the island of Manhattan grew from 60,000 to over 200,000. This rapid growth led to overcrowding and poor sanitary conditions. Those who could afford it sought refuge for themselves and their families off the island and north of Manhattan along the east bank of the Hudson River. The area, now known as the Bronx, was one of the first communities to be used as such a refuge. With the advent of Fulton's steamboat in 1807, access to the Hudson Valley also became easier.

The origins of Wave Hill date back to the 1830's. Initially, Wave Hill consisted of just one estate built by William Lewis Morris in 1843. A lawyer and grandnephew of a signer of the Declaration of Independence, Morris built a fieldstone, Greek Revival house and lived there with his six children into the 1850's. In 1864, William Henry Appleton bought the property and redesigned the house, making it larger and more Victorian. Appleton, a Boston-born publisher, was also interested in science and horticulture. In addition to being the publisher of Darwin's "Origin of Species", he had frequent guests such as T. H. Huxley (a booster of Darwin) and John Tyndall (a physicist who was one of the first to consider the effect of greenhouse gases). Under Appleton's guidance, many of the gardens were built at Wave Hill. For several summers, Appleton and his heirs rented the house to Samuel Clemens and Teddy Roosevelt's parents. The house and gardens of Wave Hill were eventually bought by George Perkins in 1903 in an effort to expand his own abutting estate, Glyndor, to 80 acres.

George Perkins (1862-1920) was born in Chicago and worked for the New York Life Insurance Company from an early age rather than attend high school. In the 1890's, Perkins was promoted with a move to New York after improving the profitability of New York Life by reorganizing the manner in which agents were paid. He then purchased the estate adjacent to Wave Hill, and he named it Glyndor. While at New York Life, his success was noticed by J. P. Morgan, who offered him a job at ten times his New York Life salary - an offer he declined given his loyalty to New York Life. When Teddy Roosevelt became governor of New York, he named Perkins to head up the Palisades Interstate Park Commission which was formed to save the Palisades from quarrying and development. (Perkins's interest in saving the Palisades was motivated by : his view of the Palisades from Glyndor, and the fact that the quarrying with its dynamite explosions would awake his daughter from her naps). Seeking funding for the preservation of the Palisades, Perkins approached J. P. Morgan for a contribution. Morgan agreed to contribute if Perkins would agree to become a partner at Morgan's bank. This time Perkins agreed. As a partner at Morgan's, he was instrumental in organizing the consolidation of International Harvester and the United States Steel Corporation. In 1910, he left Morgan's to assist Teddy Roosevelt in the formation of the Progressive Party and to pursue other interests such as the modernization of industry (cooperation vs. competition), employees benefits and conservation.

The Perkins family lived at Glyndor and leased out Wave Hill. When Perkins purchased Glyndor in 1895, he hired C. Grant Lafarge to redesign and substantially increase the size of the existing house. As the father of four children, he also added a swimming pool and a recreation center with squash courts, a bowling alley, and billiard tables, etc. (now the ecology center). He also expanded the greenhouses and enhanced the views of the Hudson and the Palisades beyond by clearing trees and adding several terraces. Perkins died in 1920, and six years later, Glyndor was struck by lightning, badly damaged, and therefore torn down. Perkins' wife rebuilt a smaller Georgian style house on that site that is now open to the public as an art gallery.

After the death of a long-term tenant in 1928, Perkins' daughter took possession of the Wave Hill house and remodeled the house by removing its Victorian architecture to make it more Georgian in style. In 1960, the Perkins family deeded the two houses (Glyndor and Wave Hill) plus 28 acres of gardens and greenhouses to the city of New York to be known as "Wave Hill". The entire garden is maintained by the city of New York and open to the public every day except Mondays. Garden and history tours are available and free with the price of admission, and the two houses are also open for self guided tours. Neither house has furnishings, but Glyndor has an art gallery, and Wave Hill has a cafeteria with access to the terraces behind the house. The views of the Hudson from the terraces and gardens are open and include the skyline of New York City. Visitors can enjoy a variety of gardens including an aquatic garden, a monocot garden, a wild garden and a flower garden. Plants and trees generally are well-marked and varied. Many of the greenhouses are open for viewing, and there is over 1/2 mile of woodland trails to hike and explore.

Wave Hill

UNTERMYER PARK AND GARDENS

945 North Broadway, Yonkers, NY 10701
Website: www.untermyer.org
Phone: 914-613-4562
Season: Year round
Days and Hours of Operation: 7 AM to sunset
Tours: Horticultural and Historical Tours given on Sundays from late April to early November (check website for times).
Entry Fees: Free to the Gardens: Tour Fees $10 or $ 20 depending on tour (check website)

Located in and owned by the City of Yonkers, Untermyer Park and Garden occupies 43 acres on the banks of the Hudson with a view of the Palisades beyond. In 1862, John Waring, an industrialist, purchased this property and built the mansion called "Greystone". The estate was then sold to Samuel Tilden, who at that time was a retired governor of New York and an unsuccessful candidate for president against Rutherford B. Hayes. In 1899, Samuel Untermyer purchased the estate and over the ensuing years increased its size to 150 acres which he covered with gardens and greenhouses. Since gardens and horticulture were his second passion, he employed 60 gardeners to maintain the property. Untermyer loved the beauty, the experimentation and the science of horticulture. Unlike most of his wealthy contemporaries, he was actively involved with not only the design of his gardens, but with the cultivation of his plants. Horticulture was a means for him to relax from the very busy and contentious life of the practice of law - his first passion.

Samuel was the child of Bavarian-Jewish immigrants and grew up in

Lynchburg, VA where his father owned a dry goods store and a textile company that made uniforms for the Confederacy. As a result of some bad investments in tobacco, his father went bankrupt and died in 1866. His mother, at the same time, had invested in real estate and, before the Civil War, sent $10,000 worth of gold coins to New York City for safekeeping. At the death of Samuel's father, the family moved to New York and eventually Samuel joined his half-brother in the practice of law after graduating from Columbia Law School at age 20. In 1883, he defended a German-American brewer successfully, acting as a sole litigator for 106 hours against a team of five Anglo-Saxon lawyers. This case made Samuel and his firm the "go-to" firm in New York. Realizing the rewards of litigation were limited, in the 1890's, the firm started to do corporate law and worked with corporate leaders like William Rockefeller and Randolph Hearst to develop trusts. Frequently, the firm was paid in stock in lieu of money, and Samuel became an astute investor. In 1910, he was paid $775,000 ($19 million today) for arranging the merger of the Boston Consolidated Copper Company and the Utah Copper Company.

During the early 1900's, Samuel's politics became more progressive and reformist, after realizing that the trusts were hurting the "little guy" as well as the economy. In 1913, he was appointed lead counsel to the Pujo Committee - a U.S. Congressional committee formed to investigate the activities of the financial trusts on Wall Street led by J. P. Morgan, George Baker and James Stillman. Serious abuses were identified in the banking clearing houses and the stock exchanges, and the need for controls became clear. As a result of the findings of the Pujo Committee, the 16th Amendment (income tax), the Federal Reserve Act, and the Clayton Antitrust Act were passed.

Prior to his tenure on the Pujo Committee, Samuel had decided to retire from his law firm, but he continued to be drawn into the legal arena. In the 1930's, he saw the threat of Hitler's Nazi Party and predicted that eventually Hitler would invoke the mass destruction of the Jews. For this reason, in the 1930's he organized a boycott of German goods and services in the United States until he became ill in 1938. He died in 1940.

Samuel hoped that the state of New York would make "Greystone" a state park and maintain the property and its gardens for the public good.

Unfortunately, the state rejected his wish and the property was in limbo until 1946 when the city of Yonkers accepted 16 acres of the original 150 acres as a city park and in the 1990's an additional 27 acres were added. The house "Greystone" has been torn down, but the gardens are in the process of being restored. Recently completed was the "Temple of Love", a temple that sits on a rock promontory with a rock garden and cascading falls below. Trails from the "Temple of Love" lead onto a woodland trail to an overlook of the Hudson flanked by two ancient Roman columns. Another approach to the overlook is a staircase passing through an allée that leads from the Walled Garden. The Walled Garden, which Untermyer referred to as "The Greek Garden" (although many feel it is the finest example of a Persian garden in the western hemisphere) is surrounded by crenellated walls with corner towers. Within the garden are criss-crossing canals, and at the north end of the garden is a Greek amphitheater flanked by sphinxes set on columns. On the west is a Grecian temple that features a spectacular view of the Hudson.

Walled Garden at Untermyer Park

■ LYNDHURST

635 South Broadway, Tarrytown, NY 10591
Website: www.lyndhurst.org
Phone: 914-631-4481
Season: April through October. Closed in November until Thanksgiving
    weekend and open in December
Days and Hours of Operation: Thursday through Monday 10 AM to 4 PM
Tour Fees: Different Tours offered ($16-$20)-check website for details

Lyndhurst is a 67-acre estate (originally 426 acres) on the Hudson River just south of Kykuit. Its history dates back to 1838 when William Paulding, Jr. (1770-1854) hired Alexander Jackson Davis to design a country villa to escape to. The design of the house was unusual in that it was Gothic with turrets, stained glass and asymmetric lines. Paulding had grown up in Tarrytown and sought the tranquility of the countryside as an escape from his legal work and his career as two-time mayor of New York, a Brigadier General in the War of 1812 and two terms in the U.S. House of Representatives.

After Paulding's death in 1854, the property was purchased by George Merritt (1807-1873). Merritt had achieved initial financial success with stores in Manhattan, but made his fortune when he bought the patent for railcar springs. Prior to that time, riding on a railroad car was fast but very uncomfortable. He became the sole manufacturer of this spring at a time when the railroads were beginning their boom, and this became the source of his fortune. Unlike Paulding, Merritt wanted Lyndhurst to be a sign that he had achieved great financial success. With this goal, he rehired the original architect to double the size of the house in 1864. This was done by adding a wing to the north and a five story tower, while preserving the footprint of the original house. As an amateur horticulturalist, Merritt also took more interest in the grounds and gardens. He selectively cleared the woodlands, making way for open lawns in front of the house and allowing views of the river from the rear of the house. He also planted many exotic trees, created gardens and built a glass and wooden conservatory that burned to the ground in 1880. Merritt died in 1873, only eight years after the renovation of the house.

Jay Gould (1836-1892) bought the house in 1880 not only as an expression of his wealth, but also as a safe place for his wife, six children and himself. The son of a bankrupt farmer in the Catskills of New York, at an early age he set off on his own and while working, educated himself in surveying and mathematics. Initially in the surveying and later tanning business, he began to purchase and refurbish small family railroads and then sell them for a profit. Between 1866 and 1868, he was involved in the Erie War (the battle between Gould and Cornelius Vanderbilt to take control of the failing Erie Railroad). Gould and his compatriots prevailed by conspiring with Boss Tweed and by bribing many in the New York legislature to allow him to water down the stock of the Erie Railroad. In 1869, Gould and his comrades decided to corner the market on gold in order to devalue the dollar, thus making grain more attractive to foreign investors, so more of it would be shipped on his railroads. To make this conspiracy work, the officials of the federal government (the Grant administration) had to agree that they would not sell any gold. This agreement was reached secretly with bribes, but when the bribed officials reneged, the financial markets failed, causing the "Black Friday of 1869". Fortunately for Gould, he was notified of the government's change of heart and sold his gold before the crash at a great profit. By 1886, Gould was one of the richest men in the world: he owned the rapid transit system of New York City, Western Union and as many miles of railroad as Vanderbilt.

He was rich, but because of his involvement in the Erie War and the "Black Friday of 1869", he was also hated. Therefore, Lyndhurst was a place where he and his family were heavily guarded. Despite his ethical shortcomings, Gould was very interested in horticulture and after the conservatory burned down in 1880, he engaged Lord and Burnham to build the first steel conservatory. Not only was it the largest conservatory in the United States, but it was designed with a dome to mimic the Gothic style of the house. Within the greenhouse, there were 14 different climate zones to optimize the growth of different species.

Gould died from complications of TB in 1892. Lyndhurst was then purchased from his estate by his oldest daughter, Helen, and after her death in 1938, her youngest sister Anna - the Duchess of Talleyrand - took possession of the estate. Anna rarely lived there, since her home base was at the Plaza Hotel in New York City. In 1961, the estate with all its art work, furnishings and contents was given to the National Trust.

Lyndhurst is open for tours April through December, and the grounds are open dawn to dusk. As days, hours, and ticket prices vary throughout the season, please see their website www.lyndhurst.org for the most current information. The contents of the house are original and date back to Paulding's time with all 50 pieces of the original furniture designed by Alexander Davis. Gould's library is intact, as is his collection of European art. The views of the Hudson are expansive, and the grounds and trees are well maintained. There is a large rose garden arranged in concentric circles with over 250 varieties of modern and heirloom roses. The conservatory was closed to conserve oil in World War II, and the glass has been destroyed, but the framework is intact and visitors may walk through it.

Lyndhurst

KYKUIT-THE ROCKEFELLER ESTATE

Kykuit-Philipsburg Manor Visitor Center, 381 N. Broadway, Sleepy Hollow, NY 10591
Website:www.hudsonvalley.org/historic-sites/kykuit
Phone: 914-366-6900
Season; Early May - mid November
Hours and Days of Operation: Thursdays through Sundays
Days of House Tours: Thursday through Sundays
Entry Fees: $23-$40 depending on tour

Kykuit (meaning lookout in Dutch) is located in Pocantico Hills, NY and looks over the Hudson River from a hill set back from the river. It was the family seat of John D. Rockefeller where 5 generations of the family have lived and continue to live.

As the founder of the Standard Oil Company, John D. Rockefeller (Senior) may have been the richest man in the United States in 1893. Living in New York City, he decided he needed a place in the country to which he could escape. Consequently, he started to purchase property in the hills above the Hudson with an initial purchase of 60 acres of land. He spent the weekends there in a renovated farmhouse. In 1902, the farmhouse burned down, and Senior engaged the architectural firm of Delano and Aldrich to build him a modest house with a budget of $100,000. It was Senior's and his wife's desire that the house not be showy or ostentatious, as they were religious and very conservative in their moral views, insisting that their children not smoke, drink, gamble or dance. Senior had very specific ideas regarding the design of the ground floor of this weekend retreat, but left the planning of the rest of the house to the architects and to their fourth child and only son, John D. Rockefeller (Junior).

Junior, a recent graduate of Brown and married to Abby Aldrich, worked for his father at Standard Oil in a job that was poorly defined and stressful for him, because the opportunities to prove himself were few. Taking control of the construction of this house and the development of the estate offered him this opportunity. Unfortunately, his vision of the house and gardens was different from his father's. Junior wanted the world to understand that the Rockefellers embraced beauty and taste, rather than just money and power. His father, however, just wanted something that was practical. Design of the house began in 1905, and it was ready for use in 1908. Unfortunately, there were problems with the house. The plumbing, furnaces and elevators were noisy, the guests' and servants' rooms were cramped and there were no closets. In 1909, the design of the house was reworked with the input of William Welles Bosworth (the original planner the gardens) and Ogden Codman (an architect and the designer of the interior of the original house). A 4th floor was added and the 3rd floor expanded to better accomodate visiting family and guests. The front of the house was pushed out and the original sloping roof of the third and fourth floors was squared off. Essentially, the squaring of the house transformed it from a very large farmhouse to an Italian villa. The renovation was completed in 1913, and Senior and his wife Laura (called Cettie), moved back in. The gardens were also completed that year under the direction of Bosworth. It seems that Senior was happy with the finished product that Junior had so conscientiously overseen, although disappointed with the cost. The cost of the house was $1,115,555 (budget was around $100,000) and the garden was $1,360,413 (budget was $30,000).

In 1915, Senior's wife, Cettie, died and Senior lived alone in the house overseeing a staff of 200 in the house, garden and fields until his death in 1937. Before his death, Senior had added about 3,000 acres to the estate to protect his view, developed 20 miles of roads, built a 9-hole golf course, and constructed over 90 houses for workers and their families. Junior and Abby took possession of the house in 1937, but by that time, their own children had grown up. As the years passed, they spent less time there, preferring a small house in Williamsburg, Virginia as well as houses in Seal Harbor, Maine and Arizona. Abby died unexpectedly in 1948, and Junior followed in 1960, having sold the estate to his children in 1951 for $760,295.

While Kycuit remained jointly owned by Junior's sons, only Nelson was interested in making it his residence. Nelson Rockefeller, Abby and Junior's son, was a patron of modern art, governor of New York, and became Vice President of the United States under Gerald Ford. In 1962, he moved in after renovating the house and finding space in the gardens for his modern sculpture collection and more space for his art collection in the unused passageways of Kykuit. His renovations were limited, and he kept many of the furnishings of his father and grandfather, because eventually he wanted the house to be open to the public as a place where the Rockefellers' history and the family contributions could be better understood. Married for the second time, Nelson was the first to raise children in Kykuit, and many of the changes to the house and gardens were done to accommodate their needs. After an illustrious career, Nelson died unexpectedly on Jan 26, 1979. In his will, he left Kykuit to the National Trust for Historic Preservation. Legally, he had no right to do this, as he owned the estate jointly with his two remaining brothers - David and Lawrence. Both opposed the idea of making Kykuit a museum, but both realized that maintenance of Kykuit as a private estate was impractical. After a long period of negotiation between the Rockefeller Brothers' Fund, Rockefeller University and the National Trust, a solution was found. Much of the 3,000 acres was given to the state of New York to form Rockefeller State Park, and ownership of the house was given to the National Trust with the management of the estate residing with the Rockefeller Brothers' Fund. Although many of the family still live on the estate, Kykuit was opened to the public in 1994.

Kykuit is open to the public by guided tour only, and days of touring are limited. With several choices of tours, the visitor needs to be selective according to their interests as it is not possible to see everything in the house, gardens and art collections in the two hours allotted. The house is shown as it was left in 1979 and the contents reflect the three generations who lived there. Nelson's art and sculpture collection are in tact. The views of the Hudson Valley are magnificent, and the gardens are extensive. Since the house is built on a hill, the gardens are terraced and organized in a sequence of garden rooms. The classical gardens feature garden statuary, pergolas, pools and temples.

Kykuit

BOSCOBEL HOUSE AND GARDENS

1601 NY-9D, Garrison, NY 10524
Website: www.boscobel.org
Phone: 845-265-3638
Season: April through December
Hours and Days of Operation: Wednesday-Monday 9:30-5 PM (closed
    Tuesdays)
House Tours: 10-4 PM
Admission Fees: $17 Adult / $14 Seniors / $8 Children 6-14 / Children under
    6 free

Boscobel, meaning "Beautiful Woods" in Italian, overlooks the
Hudson River and West Point beyond. It encompasses over 100 acres of
gardens, orchards and pathways that lead into the woods and overlook
Constitution Island and its surrounding marshes. Located in Garrison,
New York, the estate was rescued from demolition in the mid-1950's when
it was moved from Montrose, New York to its present site.

The construction of Boscobel originated with States Morris
Dyckman. Born in 1755, into a family perpetually in debt and of low social
status, Dyckman became successful as a Loyalist in the Revolutionary
War by serving in the Quartermaster Corps of the British army in New
York City. From 1781 to 1789, Dyckman, under Quartermaster General
Erskine, spent time in England to help his supervisors explain charges of
fraud. In charge of accounts, he was able to clear himself and others. On
returning to his farm in New York in 1789, he received a large annuity
funded by a grateful General Erskine. Expecting to live out his years as
a "gentleman farmer", he fell into debt, and when Erskine died, his heirs

refused to pay the annuity. Dyckman returned to England in 1800 to get his annuity, and while there, he essentially blackmailed other members of the Quartermaster Corps by threatening to expose their wrongdoing during the Revolutionary War. In return for destroying incriminating records, he received a payment of at least 28,500 pounds ($3.8 million today), and his annuity was restored. He returned to the United States in 1803 with a plan to construct a Federalist-style house, and in 1804, construction on the house began.

Unfortunately, Dyckman died in 1806 before the house was completed, but his family and heirs lived at Boscobel until 1888, running the estate as an active farm.

From 1888 to 1923, the estate suffered a gradual decline. In 1923, the property was purchased as a public park by Westchester County, but because of the Depression and World War II, little was done about the house and land. In 1945, the property including the house was purchased by the Veteran's Administration, and 32 buildings were erected on the original farm, leaving the original house intact but under threat of being razed. In 1955, the Veteran's Administration sold the house for demolition for $35. After being stripped of its architectural details, the house was to be demolished, but was saved when a group of concerned citizens obtained a court injunction to halt demolition, then raised enough money to purchase 60 acres on the Hudson in Garrison, New York and moved the house to this new site. By 1961, with the financial support of caring benefactors, including Lila Wallace, the co-founder of Reader's Digest, Boscobel's restoration was completed and opened to the public as a museum of decorative arts.

The house and gardens are open six days a week from April through December. The house is available for viewing with a guided tour. Most contents of the house are not original, but represent the best Neoclassical furnishings made and available in New York between 1800-1820 including masterpieces by Duncan Phyfe and other New York cabinet makers. The design of the gardens and grounds is not original. In the 1800's, the estate was a working farm with a cutting and herb garden. Today, the landscape design is more symmetrical and classical. A maple allée leads to a squared-off forecourt. On either side of the driveway is an orchard and to the north of the house is a rose garden, herb garden and orangery. Behind the house, symmetrical pathways lead down to a hidden terrace with spectacular views of the Hudson River, Constitution Island and West Point. There is also a woodland trail. Finally, there are guided grounds tours and recorded audio tours available which describe the history of the area as well as the importance of the Hudson River.

Boscabel's view of the Hudson

■ STONECROP GARDENS

81 Stonecrop Lane, Cold Spring, NY 10516
Website: www.stonecrop.org
Phone: 845-265-2000
Season: April-October
Hours and Days of Operation: Monday through Saturday and select Sundays,
    10-5 PM
House Tours: NO TOURS as the house is private
Entry Fees: $5

Located on hills adjacent to the east side of the Hudson River and near Cold Spring, New York, Stonecrop is a 15 acre garden created by Anne and Frank Cabot. Built as a weekend retreat, Stonecrop evolved into a nursery business and eventually into a public garden. The property was a gift in the 1950's from Anne's grandmother, Evelina Ball Perkins, the wife of George W. Perkins (1862-1920) who was a self-made man and a partner of J.P. Morgan. Perkins also acquired several properties along the Hudson River including "Wave Hill", and as President of the Palisades Interstate Park Commission, he was instrumental in preserving the Hudson Palisades from quarrying. Anne's parents were also conservationists and on their death, they left their 957-acre farm, Glynwood, which was adjacent to Stonecrop, to a non-profit organization dedicated to rural conservation.

Frank Cabot was brought up in New York City, and after serving in World War II, completed Harvard College in 1949. He then went to work in New York at Stone and Webster, an engineering and investment banking firm, and then at Train, Cabot, and Associates as a venture capitalist. While in New York, weekends were spent initially at Glynwood, Anne's family's farm. In 1958 they built a weekend house at Stonecrop, and with a strong interest in alpine plants, the Cabots hired Rex Murfitt and opened an alpine nursery. Gradually, the property evolved from 40 acres of woodlands and fields to include the house, horse fields, a perennial garden and a nursery. When Mr Cabot retired in 1976, the gardens were expanded with the plan that they would ultimately become a public garden which would be both educational and inspirational for aspiring gardeners. This became a reality in 1992.

Frank Cabot died in 2011 at age 86. Stonecrop was not his only legacy to the horticultural world. During his lifetime, he added to and refined the existing gardens of over 20 acres on his family's estate, "Quatre Vents" on the St. Lawrence River looking over the Laurentian Mountains of Canada. This endeavor is beautifully described in his book, "The Greater Perfection". In addition, in the late 1980's, concerned that important American gardens would be lost to development and neglect, Cabot founded the Garden Conservancy in Garrison, New York whose goal was the preservation of these endangered gardens.

Tours of Stonecrop are self-guided, and the gardens are open Monday through Saturday, 10 AM to 5 PM. One enters the garden through a floating glass 2,000-square foot conservatory, and garden maps and a plant list are provided on arrival. Stonecrop, a plant enthusiast's garden, incorporates a diverse collection of gardens and plants, including woodland and water gardens, raised alpine stone beds, cliff rock gardens and an enclosed English-style flower garden, among other horticultural delights. Plants are also available for purchase.

Conservatory at Stonecrop

LOCUST GROVE ESTATE

2683 South Road, Poughkeepsie NY 12601
Web Site: lgny.org
Telephone: 845-454-4500
Season: April to December
Days and Hours of Operation: Weekends only in April, November and
    December: Daily from May through October 10 AM to 5 PM
Entry Fees: $11 Adults/ $6 for youths (6-18)

Located in Poughkeepsie, New York on the banks of the Hudson River, Locust Grove is a 200-acre estate with a park-like landscape, gardens and a house that was the passion of Samuel F. B.Morse, the inventor of the telegraph.

Samuel was born in 1791 in Charlestown, Massachusetts to a clergyman and author of geography books. On his graduation from Yale in 1810 and with the recommendations of Gilbert Stuart and Benjamin West, he convinced his parents to underwrite a year of study at London's Royal Academy of Art. He studied with these two artists and painted "The Dying Hercules" that was much acclaimed by the British, but not well-received by the Americans. On returning to the United States, he became an itinerant portrait painter who supported himself by finding commissions in Charleston, South Carolina, New York City and in Washington, DC.. In 1816, he married and started a family who were forced to live in New Haven with his parents while he sought portrait subjects to paint in other cities. Missing his family and realizing that the rewards of portrait painting would not enable him to reunite with his family, he began to invent machines that he hoped would bring him his fortune. Morse invented a water pump for fire engines and a machine that carved marble, but both ventures failed. In 1825, his future as an artist brightened when his portrait of the Marquis de Lafayette was met with great success. This success enabled him to travel to Europe, and on one of these trips, a conversation with a fellow traveler about electricity gave him the idea for the telegraph. In 1832, Morse began work on its development, and by 1840, he had a patent for the telegraph. Four years later, a demonstration line between Washington, D.C. and Baltimore proved the value of the telegraph as a means of long-distance communication. At that time, Morse realized that this invention would make him a rich man and allow him to settle down and purchase a home for his family.

In 1847, he bought Locust Grove with its 100 acres of farmland which had been farmed by the Livingston family and its descendants since the early 1700's. As an artist, Samuel reconfigured the approach to the house by planting both local and exotic trees in a more "picturesque style". He also transformed the original Federal style house to a Tuscan style house by adding a four-story tower, a porte cochere and two octagonal wings. He accomplished this with the help of the architect Alexander Jackson Davis, and on its completion, the mansion measured 14,000 square feet. Samuel lived there with his seven children until his death in 1872. His second wife continued to use the house until the 1890's, when she rented the house to the Young family from Poughkeepsie. They eventually bought and modernized the house in 1901. In an effort to perpetuate their family legacy as well as Samuel Morse's legacy, the Young family created a not-for-profit foundation to preserve the estate for the benefit of the public in 1975.

The house is open for tours on a daily basis from April to December. None of the contents belonged to the Morse family, but are original to the Young family. Most of the mansion's 25 rooms are open for touring including the kitchen in the basement of the the house. The landscape is well-preserved and has been expanded to over 200 acres. Views of the Hudson are limited, but there are hiking trails down to the Hudson. The gardens are well-maintained and reflect the efforts of Martha Young. The garden is about one-half acre, rectangular and organized by plant species.

There is also an extensive vegetable garden. The approach to the house, as designed by Morse, is park-like and obscures the view of the house until you come upon it. At the front of the property is visitor's center where one can view a video of Morse's life and the history of Locust Grove. There is also a gallery of Morse's paintings, mostly portraits, a discussion of his artistic career, as well as an explanation of the telegraph.

Locust Grove - Courtesy of Nathaniel Cooper and Locust Grove

INNISFREE GARDEN

362 Tyrrel Road, Millbrook, NY 12545
Website: innisfreegarden.org
Phone: 845-677-8000
Season: Early May to Mid October
Days and Hours of Operation: Wednesday through Friday 10 AM to 4 PM
Entry Fees: $6 Adults/ Free to children under 3

Innisfree is located in Millbrook, New York, 15 miles east of the Hudson River. It is composed of a series of gardens without artificial barriers that flow together in a park-like setting. After marrying late in life in 1922, Walter Beck (1864-1954) and his wife Marion (1876-1959) created Innisfree in the late 1920's, after Marion's father, an iron magnate, left her a great deal of money as well as the 950 acres of the land where Innisfree is located. Independently wealthy, they built a Queen Anne-style mansion which overlooked 40-acre Tyrrel Lake, and then proceeded to develop English gardens with terraces leading down to the lake. On a trip to London, they discovered the illustrations of an 8th century Chinese garden designed by Wong Wei, a poet, painter and garden designer. Realizing that the natural setting of their property with its cliffs, rock outcroppings, streams and lake was more amenable to a Chinese design than the structure of English gardens, they discarded their original plans for the gardens. Of particular interest to them was the Chinese concept of a "cup garden" - a garden which is designed to highlight a rare and special natural object without distractions from its surroundings.

This concept may have been particularly appealing to Walter as prior to his involvement with the gardens at Innisfree, he was an artist, sculptor, and muralist. Having grown up in Dayton, Ohio, next to a home for Civil War veterans, his interest in art started with his drawings of stories told to him by the veterans. He went on to study at the Royal Academy of Fine Art in Munich, and much of his work focused on figures of the Civil War and maritime scenes.

Many of Walter's cup gardens focused on the naturally sculpted elements of the property such as rock outcroppings, stone stairways, streams, a plant, trees and boulders. Most of the original garden development took place around the house and north of the lake. Marion focused more on the placement and selection of plant material. In 1938, the Becks met Lester Collins (1914-1993) at a lecture on Chinese gardens at Harvard. This meeting initiated a lifelong collaboration between Collins and the Becks. Collins was then a student, but eventually joined the Harvard faculty and in 1954, became the Dean of the Harvard Graduate School of Design. From 1938 until his death in 1993, he worked with the Becks and later with the Innisfree Foundation to further refine the gardens.

Walter died at age 90 in 1954, and Marion died after a long illness in 1959. It had been the Beck's intent to establish a foundation to maintain Innisfree for the enjoyment and education of the public, but unfortunately Marion's illness had taken its toll financially, and there was no money left to fund the foundation. However, a foundation was formed through private donations and by the sale of over 750 acres of the estate to Rockefeller University as an environmental and scientific center. Despite some financial restrictions, Collins continued to refine the gardens by sculpting the land with the use of berms and natural pathways, thereby optimizing flow between Walter's cup gardens. In addition, he developed a walkway around the lake by grassing over gravel roads and establishing a bridge over Tyrrel Lake. After dredging the lake, Collins used the mud to resculpt the shoreline of the lake. By tearing down the mansion in 1972 and reducing the number of workers from 20 to 6, he also was successful in reducing the cost of running the garden. At his death in 1993, Collin's wife took over and was instrumental in adding more plant variety to the garden.

The garden is open Tuesday - Sunday from 10-4. Admission is $6 and there are no amenities at the garden except Port-a-Potties. A booklet with a map and an explanation of the gardens are provided with the price of admission. Circumnavigation of the lake is ambitious for those with bad knees, but the walk to the site of the original house is reasonable and represents the core of the garden with its terraces, waterfalls, streams, bridges, steps, natural sculptures and beautiful trees including oaks, ginkgos, willows, Japanese maples and clipped pears. Views of the lake are varied and interspersed with sculptured vistas and are enhanced by sunlight streaming through the trees.

WETHERSFIELD

88 Wethersfield Way, Amenia, NY 12501
Website: www.wethersfieldgarden.org
Phone: 845-373-8073
Season: June through September
Days and Hours of Operation: Garden only:Thursday through Saturday Noon
    to 5pm; Garden, Carriage House, and Main House: 2 tours on Thursday
    through Saturday-call for reservations.
Entry Fees: Garden only-$5; House, Carriage House and Garden Tours-$20
    Adults/ $15 Seniors and Students (13-18)/ Children under 12 -Free

Wethersfield is an estate of 1,200 acres and lies about 20 miles east of the Hudson River in Amenia, New York, an area of rolling hills that supports farming, wineries and horse farms.

Chauncey Devereux Stillman discovered this area in 1937 while riding in a fox hunt. Mr. Stillman (1907-1989) was the grandson of James Stillman, who parlayed his father's Texas banking and railroad interests into a controlling interest of the National City Bank of New York (now CitiBank). With the premature death of his father and brother, Chauncey inherited the bulk of his grandfather's fortune before he graduated from Harvard in 1929. Following Harvard, he attended Columbia Architecture School and subsequently pursued his interests in fox hunting, sailing (Commodore of the New York Yacht Club), art collecting and calligraphy since there was no need for him to join the world of commerce.

Given his love for horses and fox hunting, he purchased a dairy farm in Amenia, and, as a first step, proceeded to build the stables for what was to become a large estate of 1,200 acres. In 1939, he married, an event that led to the necessity for the construction of a Georgian-style house (the architect was Bancel LaFarge) at the highest point on his new estate. Unfortunately, the marriage only lasted 10 years, but did produce two daughters. Following his divorce, Chauncey kept Wethersfield, living both there and in an apartment in New York City. At Wethersfield, he continued to pursue his love of horses by raising Hackney horses used for pulling his collection of carriages. In addition, he continued to work with landscape architects Bryan Lynch and Evelyn Poehler to build, extend and then refine the classical gardens that encompass over ten acres at Wethersfield. Mr. Stillman died in 1989 after creating the Homeland Foundation whose purpose, among others, was to maintain Wethersfield's gardens, stables, farms, house and art collection for the benefit of the public.

Tours of the estate are available and need to be arranged prior to a visit. Starting at the stables, the tour includes a viewing of Mr. Stillman's collection of 22 beautifully restored carriages and their accoutrements. The tour then moves to the top of the hill for a viewing of the house. Georgian in style, the house borders the garden which provides magnificent views of rolling fields and the mountains beyond. The contents of the house are original and contain antiques belonging to Chauncey's grandfather and parents. They range from Chippendale to Louis XV and XVI furniture. With an extensive art collection, the house contains the works of Toulouse-Lautrec, Ingres, Thayer, Degas, Sargent, Gilbert Stuart and many others. In addition to the paintings, there are two dramatic frescoes by Pietro Annigoni.

Tours of the garden are self-guided and facilitated by a map and the usual presence of gardeners happy to answer questions. The ten acres of gardens are extensive and classical in design with inclusion of pools and fountains, sculptures, terraces and garden rooms. The walkways are defined by hedges, topiary and sculpture and effectively create vistas that allow the eye to capture the magnificent views beyond. The garden may be toured without joining a guided tour, but hours and days are limited.

Garden at Wethersfield

HOME OF FRANKLIN D. ROOSEVELT NATIONAL HISTORIC SITE

4097 Albany Post Road, Hyde Park, NY 12538
Website: www.nps.gov/hofr
Phone: 845-229-9115
Season: Year Round
Days and Hours of Operation: Daily - 9 AM to 5 PM
Entry Fees: $18 for tour of FDR's House and Self-Guided tour of the Museum

Springwood was the estate owned by Franklin Roosevelt's family in Hyde Park, NY overlooking the Hudson River. In 1943, prior to FDR's death, it was given to the United States by Franklin Roosevelt and is now open to the public under the supervision of the National Park Service.

The history of Springwood dates back to 1672, when the English crown granted 220 square miles of land to nine businessmen who proceeded to create nine lots - each with frontage on the Hudson River. One of these lots is where Springwood now resides. In 1795, a large Federal style farmhouse was built there and remains the core of today's mansion. The house was remodeled in 1845 with the addition of a tower consistent with Italianate architecture. Franklin's father, James, purchased the estate in 1866, which at that time, encompassed 110 acres and cost $40,000. James was a man of leisure with financial interests in coal and railroads who lived the life of a country gentleman and pursued his interest in horse breeding. A widower, he married Sara Delano who was 26 years younger in 1880. In 1882, Franklin was born after a long and difficult delivery, making further pregnancies for Sara impossible.

Franklin was an active and only child who spent most of his early years at Springwood tutored by governesses, riding horses, and playing with cousins, neighbors and the children of staff before going off to boarding school at Groton at age 14. James died in 1900, leaving the bulk of his fortune and the estate to his wife.

In 1905, Franklin married his cousin, Eleanor Roosevelt, and proceeded to have six children (one of whom died in infancy). Because of Franklin's growing family and his political aspirations, the house was renovated in 1915. Two wings and a third floor were added to accommodate the children and staff. More space was added to serve as public rooms for political purposes and to accommodate Franklin's growing library and collection of stamps, naval paintings, and stuffed birds - a hobby of his. During this last renovation, the house doubled in size and was transformed architecturally into a Colonial Revival.

Throughout the Roosevelts' married life, the mansion at Hyde Park served as an anchor for Franklin and the family since his political career caused him to move around a great deal. While president, he visited Hyde Park almost 200 times and used the estate as a summer White House. He also entertained leaders of state such as Winston Churchill, King George VI and Queen Elizabeth at Springwood. His close relationship with his mother made visits to Hyde Park difficult for Eleanor. Because Sara Roosevelt controlled the purse strings, she continued to exercise a great deal of control over the running of the estate until her death in 1941. Visits to Springwood for Franklin were often stressful because of Sara's control over the estate, her uneasy relationship with her daughter-in-law and a constant stream of visitors. This led Franklin to build "Top Cottage" in 1938 as an "escape from the mob" (his words) and a place to retire. After his mother's death, Franklin began plans for a presidential library on the estate and made arrangements for the estate to be given to the National Park Service with the provision that the family have a life tenancy.

Tours of Springwood include the house, stables and gardens where FDR's grave site is located. There is also a tour of the presidential library. The guided house tour includes the first and second floor of the main house. The contents of the house are original to FDR's time and include his collection of books, paintings (especially naval paintings) and stuffed birds. At the completion of the house tour, one can wander the grounds and imagine what the original view of the Hudson looked like before being obstructed by the growth of trees (all planted by FDR, who said his second occupation was a tree farmer). Visitors are free to view the stables, gardens and Eleanor and Franklin's grave site at one's leisure. The presidential library is a short walk from the grave site, and the exhibits at the library offer a great review of modern-day history from the Great Depression through World War II. One needs at least several hours to take advantage of the library.

While you are visiting Springwood, you may want to visit the gardens of Bellefield. Now the administrative offices of the National Park Services and only a hundred yards away from the visitor center of the FDR National Historic site, the house is one of the oldest existing houses in the area. Although the house is not open to the public, the garden, designed by Beatrix Farrand in 1911, is open dawn to dusk seven days a week. The garden is a walled and private garden and one of the few remaining examples of Farrand's work which include Dumbarton Oaks in Washington, DC, the Harkness Gardens in Waterford, CT, and the Rose Garden at the New York Botanical Garden.

Springwood-FDR's home at Hyde Park

VANDERBILT MANSION NATIONAL HISTORIC SITE

119 Vanderbilt Park Road, Hyde Park, NY 12538
Website: www.nps.gov/vama
Phone: 845-229-7770
Season: Open year round
Hours and Days of operation: Daily from 9-5 PM. May vary by season-check
    the website
Days of House Tours: Daily
Fees: $!0 to $16: National Park Passes accepted

It all started with Cornelius Vanderbilt. Born in 1810, he borrowed $100 from his parents at age 16 to purchase a sailing barge to be used as a ferry between Staten Island and Manhattan. He transformed this ferry service into a major shipping line that not only serviced Europe, but also San Francisco by way of Nicaragua. With the advent of the railroad, he understood that much of his maritime business would be displaced by the faster and cheaper railroads. In the 1870's, he consolidated all his wealth into the acquisition and construction of railroads. Believing in the the law of primogeniture, at his death in 1877, he left the bulk of his fortune of $100 million to his son, William, despite having 13 children. In the 8 years following the death of his father, William was able to double the Vanderbilt fortune by expanding the railroad business. At his death in 1885, he left $195 million to his eight children. Frederick was William's seventh child, and he and his wife, Louise, built the mansion in Hyde Park as their spring and fall getaway.

Born in 1856, Frederick was the first of the Vanderbilt children to attend college (Yale) and in 1878, he married Louise despite the disapproval of his family due to her marriage of very short duration to a Vanderbilt cousin. However, by the time of William's death in 1885, Louise had become his favorite daughter-in-law, and Frederick was included in his father's will.

Frederick worked in the family business but did find time for leisure by building vacation retreats first in Newport (see Rough Point), then Hyde Park, Bar Harbor, Maine and the Adirondacks. Frederick and Louise originally built a mansion in Newport, Rhode Island (Rough Point). Because of some disagreements with Frederick's brothers and Newport's highly charged social atmosphere, they decided to find a more tranquil location, and in 1895, they purchased an existing 200 acre estate in Hyde Park from Walter Langdon, the grandson of John Jacob Astor, for $125,000. After discovering the existing mansion was unsafe for habitation, they hired Charles McKim of McKim, Mead, and White to build a neoclassical mansion overlooking the Hudson River for $2.5 million($75 million in today's dollars). The house was designed with the latest technological advances such as electricity, central heating and indoor bathrooms. It could accommodate three preferred guest couples (each with their own suite) on the second floor, and on the third floor were five more guest rooms in addition to rooms for the house servants. Frederick and Louise entertained frequently and continued to live there seasonally until Louise's death in 1926.

Frederick then spent most of his time there until his death in 1938. Childless, the estate was left to one of Frederick's nieces who had no interest in using the house and put it up for sale for $250,000. Even at that price, there was no interest in purchasing the estate due to the cost of running the estate (it required 30 servants), the Depression and income taxes. On the recommendation of FDR, the Vanderbilt's neighbor in Hyde Park, the niece gave the estate to the National Park Service as an example of the "Gilded Age". By coincidence, FDR was making arrangements to do the same with his estate in Hyde Park to serve as a place to locate the first Presidential Library.

The mansion is open daily and viewed by guided tours only. The furnishings and art are all original to the house and well-maintained.

The view of the Hudson River from the house has been obstructed by tree growth, but it is spectacular from other parts of the property. The grounds are vast and interspersed with specimen trees that in many cases are over 200 years old. The approach to the estate is intersected by a brook and falls that are crossed by a bridge. The gardens are not adjacent or visible from the house and require a walk of about 150 yards. Both Louise and Frederick enjoyed the gardens and walked there at least twice a day. Frederick was very involved with the planning of the gardens and met with his superintendent and gardener frequently. Between 1897 and 1934, three different landscape architects were involved in reworking the gardens which in some cases, dated back to the 1820's. There was also an extensive greenhouse (no longer present) that provided the Vanderbilts with plants year round.The gardens are built on a terraced hill with a garden on each of 8 different levels. At the bottom level, there is a large rose garden, and on the next level is a walled Italianate garden with a reflecting pool and pergola at one end and an allée of cherry trees at the other end.

Vanderbilt Mansion - Hyde Park

■ MONTGOMERY PLACE

55 Gardener Way, Annandale-on-the-Hudson, NY 12504
Website: www.bard.edu/montgomeryplace/visiting
Phone: 1-800-227-3665
Season: Grounds and Gardens-year round; Mansion-early June to mid October
Days and Hours of Operation: Grounds-dawn to dusk; Mansion Tours-
   Saturdays only at 10:30, 11:30, 1:30 and 2:30 (check website).
Entry Fees: Grounds-free; Mansion Tours - $10

Montgomery Place, now owned by Bard College, is located in
Annandale-on-the- Hudson, NY and is a 383-acre estate that overlooks
the Hudson River. Although now owned by the college, the basic layout
is the same as it was in 1802 when Janet Montgomery (1743-1828)
purchased the land that is bordered by the Sawkill River to the north
and the Hudson to the west. Janet was the oldest daughter of Robert
and Margaret Beekman Livingston and the older sister of Robert
"the chancellor" (see Clermont). Her husband was General Richard
Montgomery, a Revolutionary War hero, who was killed during the
Revolution at the attack of British-held Quebec in 1775. Widowed, Janet
and General Montgomery's Irish nephew created a business enterprise
with orchards, nurseries and gardens. They maintained the mills on their
property along the Sawkill, and in 1802, a Federal style house was built
with views of the Hudson and the Catskills beyond. Janet and her nephew
ran the farm together until his death in 1815, and in 1828, Janet died at
85, leaving the farm to her youngest brother, Edward Livingston.

Edward had no interest in running Montgomery Place as a commercial
enterprise as he was a public figure serving as Andrew Jackson's

Secretary of State (1831-1833) and ambassador to France (1833-1835). As a result, he deemphasized the agricultural and milling aspects of the estate and reconstituted the estate as a summer retreat, emphasizing the development of the natural landscape through the construction of roadways, paths, arboretums and views. In 1836, he died and his widow, Louise, and his daughter, Cora continued the transformation of the farm to a country estate. It is probable that in the 1840's the landscape gardener and author, Andrew Jackson Downing, contributed to the development of the property as he was a frequent visitor and friend as suggested by frequent complimentary references to Montgomery Place in his book on landscape gardening - "A Treatise on the Theory and Practice of Landscape Gardening". During this period, Louisa and Cora worked with the architect, Alexander Jackson Davis, to enlarge and redesign the Federal style house built in 1802 to that of a Neoclassical country house. In 1839, a conservatory was added. By the time Cora died in 1873, Montgomery Place had become a romantic-period showplace with a picturesque landscape.

After Cora's death in 1873, two unmarried cousins held the property in a life tenancy until 1921. During this 50 year period, the conservatory collapsed and the gardens and trails grew over as Cora's two cousins did not have the resources to maintain the estate. In 1921, Violetta and John Ross Delafield (a Livingston descendant) inherited the estate and with Violetta's interest in botany, created new gardens, restored the trails and views as well as the orchards and arboretum. In 1986, their son, Dennis Delafield turned the estate over to Historic Hudson Valley, and Bard College took over the ownership and stewardship of Montgomery Place in 2016.

The grounds of Montgomery Place are open to the public from dawn until dusk. One enters the property on a straight driveway through the orchards until the visitor's center is reached. At the visitor's center, there are restrooms, brochures with maps and displays with interpretative information. The walk from the visitor's center to the house follows along a curved, graveled driveway with lawns on either side which are interspersed with trees and passes the coach house, greenhouse and gardens to the left of the greenhouse. The house is only open on Saturdays from early June to mid October, and viewing is by guided tour only. The land behind the house is terraced and looks down toward the Hudson and onto the Catskills. Pathways then lead visitors to the formal gardens and greenhouses. The gardens include a rough garden that descends and ascends along a trail through a small gorge planted with native plants. The rough garden ends at the ellipse garden centered by a small pool in a woodland area. Nearby and next to the greenhouse, are a rose garden and a parterre herb garden and further west towards the Hudson is a perennial garden. There are also hiking trails that lead through the arboretum down to the Sawkill, the lake, the falls and the Hudson.

Looking from the porch onto the Hudson at Montgomery Place

BLITHEWOOD GARDEN

75 Blithewood Road, Annandale-on the Hudson, NY 12504
Website: inside.bard.edu/arboretum/gardens
Phone: 845-752-5323 (Arboretum voicemail); 845-758-7179 (Horticulture
   Office)
Season: Year round
Hours and Dates of Operation: No house tour; grounds open sunrise to sunset
Entry Fees: Free, $5/person suggested fee for guided group tours upon advance
   request

Located in Annandale-on- Hudson, New York, Blithewood borders Montgomery Place. Like Montgomery Place, it is owned and maintained by Bard College, and only the Italianate garden with views of the Hudson remains open for visitors. A large Georgian-style mansion built in 1899 overlooks the garden, but is not open to the public.

In 1790, John Armstrong and Alida Livingston (daughter of Robert Livingston) took possession of the 125-acre property as a working farm. A working farm tended to cluster the main house and the farm buildings together, whereas an ornamental farm (a weekend or summer retreat) would separate the main house from the farm buildings to minimize the noise, smells and activities of the farm animals. Robert Donaldson (1800-1872) and his wife purchased the farm in 1836. A gentleman from North Carolina and a man of leisure, Donaldson had come to appreciate the Romantic-era landscapes seen in the English countryside, and he intended to apply these landscape principles to his newly-purchased property. He worked with Andrew Jackson Downing (landscape architect) and Alexander Jackson Davis (architect) to implement his vision. The

Federal-style architecture of the main house was rebuilt in a more Gothic style, and the outbuildings were separated from the main residence. The landscape was transformed from a working farm to a Romantic-era landscape using the natural landscape to guide the development of the land. Removal of trees and natural features was minimized, and roadways, trails and waterways were integrated with the natural terrain. There are two types of Romantic-era landscape gardening: the beautiful or dressed landscape, and the picturesque or undressed. The dressed landscape focuses on pruning, minimizing overgrowth and the manicuring of lawns while the picturesque was wilder and more natural. Working with Donaldson, Downing created the most picturesque landscape of the Hudson Valley estates, but ultimately Blithewood was sold in 1853 to John Bard. Bard maintained the picturesque landscape as well as the main buildings, but he donated a piece of the property to found St. Stephen's College which later became Bard College in 1934.

In 1899, Captain Andrew Zabriskie (1853-1916), born to a family that owned one of the largest real estate companies in New York City, purchased the property. Married with two children, Zabriskie (1853-1916) ran the family real estate firm and pursued his passion for collecting coins, becoming a major collector of Polish and Lincoln commemorative coins. He hired Francis Hoppin (architect of The Mount and Ashintully) to redesign the grounds and gardens of Blithewood and replace the existing Gothic buildings including the main house. Only the gatehouse survived this transformation. The new mansion was Georgian in style and is now used as office and classroom space for the Levy Economics Institute of Bard. In 1966, Captain Zabriskie's son donated the garden, grounds and house to Bard College.

The garden is open to the public free of charge and is well worth the visit, given its proximity to Montgomery Place and its views of the Hudson and the Catskills beyond. There is parking next to the mansion, and the lawn overlooks the Hudson and the garden below. Located on a hill, the sunken garden is terraced and Italianate in design with many classical architectural elements. Symmetrical with geometric beds defined by boxwood hedges and brick pathways, the garden has a fountain pool at its center and a pavilion and colonnades on the riverside of the garden.

The garden at Blithewood

CLERMONT STATE HISTORIC SITE

1 Clermont Ave, Germantown, NY 12526
Website: www.parks.ny/historic-sites
Phone: 518-537-4240
Season: House Tours- mid April to mid December; Garden and Grounds-Year
    Round
Day and hours of Operation: House Tours: Mid April to End of October-
    Wednesday through Sunday 11 AM to 4 PM; November 1 to Mid
    December-Saturday and Sunday-11 AM to 3 PM
Entry Fees: $7 Adult/ $6 Seniors and Students/ $4 Children (over 12)/ Free
    Children under 12

Clermont, once a country estate of the Livingston family, is now a part of the New York State Park system. It includes the original manor house, the gardens and 500 acres of fields and forests with 5 miles of hiking trails in and around the Hudson River.

Clermont had its origins with Robert Livingston (1654-1728). Robert was born in Scotland, but because of his father's religious beliefs, was exiled to Rotterdam, Netherlands with his family at age 8. He learned Dutch and eventually emigrated to the American colonies to seek his fortune. At age 20, because of his command of the Dutch language, he became the secretary of Nicholas van Rensselaer - a Dutch patroon who owned millions of acres in the Albany area. After van Rensselaer's death, Robert married his employer's widow, had eight children, and accumulated great wealth as a fur trader, merchant and emissary of the governor of New York who, at that time, was appointed by the British crown. During his lifetime, he purchased 2,000 acres on the Hudson (where Clermont now resides) and was granted an additional 160,000 acres of land to the east of the property by the British crown for subduing a rebellion in Albany, New York (Leisler's Rebellion, 1689).

Livingston died in 1728, and his son Robert Jr. (1718-1775), a lawyer, inherited 13,000 acres (9.5 miles along Hudson River) and in 1840, built a large Georgian manor house where Clermont now stands. During his lifetime, he accumulated another 500,000 acres of land on and across the Hudson. His son, Robert "The Judge ", inherited the estate but died 5 months after his father, and the estate passed on to his son, Robert "The Chancellor" (1746-1813). Of all the Livingstons, "The Chancellor" was the most prominent. He was a drafter of the Declaration of Independence and the Constitution of the state of New York, as well as being that state's first Chancellor (head of the New York Supreme Court). As Minister of France under Thomas Jefferson, he negotiated the Louisiana Purchase. Finally, he and Robert Fulton worked together to develop the first viable steamboat. On its maiden voyage, it stopped at the dock at Clermont.

After the Chancellor died in 1813, several more generations of Livingstons lived at Clermont. In 1962, Alice Livingston gave the property with the house and its contents to the state of New York for the perpetual preservation of the land, house, and historical legacy of the family.

The 500-acre park, gardens and hiking trails are open on a daily basis, and the house is open to guided tours Wednesday to Sunday. The contents of the house are original and include portraits attributed to Gilbert Stuart and Thomas Sully (portrait of Andrew Jackson). Views from the house are of the Hudson and Catskills beyond. Created by Alice Livingston in the 1920's and 1930's, the gardens include a lilac allée, an orchard, an Italianate garden, a wilderness garden with a pool, bridge, and stream as well as a cutting garden near the old greenhouse. At the visitor's center one can learn more about the history of the Livingston family as well as the development of the steamboat.

OLANA STATE HISTORIC SITE

5720 State Route 9G, Hudson, NY 12534
Website: www.olana.org
Phone: 518-828-0135
Season: All Year
Hours and days of Operation: check website as scheduling is seasonal
Days of House Tours: check website as scheduling is seasonal
Entrance Fees: check website as fees subject to change

Olana was the home of Frederic Church from 1860 until his death in 1900. A 250 acre estate overlooking the Hudson River and Catskills beyond, it was an active farm.

In the 1860's, Frederic Church was said to be "the Michelangelo of American artists", and his success as a painter enabled him to create this estate on the Hudson River. Born in 1826 to affluent parents in Hartford, Connecticut, he showed great promise as an artist at an early age. At age 18, he went to Catskill, New York to study with Thomas Cole, the founder of the Hudson River School of Painting. After two years of training with Cole, he began a long period of travel across New England, South America, and Labrador in search of new subjects to paint. He focused on painting detailed landscapes in their most natural settings with a particular interest in the use of light. His work became immensely popular, and in 1860, he sold "The Heart of the Andes" for $10,000 ($3 million today), the most a living American painter had ever been paid for a painting. At the exhibit of that painting, he met his future wife, Isabel, and they married that same year.

Given his marriage and his financial success as a painter, Frederic purchased a 126-acre farm in Hudson, New York just across the river from where he had studied with Thomas Cole. They built a farmhouse, designed by Richard Morris Hunt, and proceeded to transform the hardscrabble farm. Thousands of trees were planted, trails and roads created, and a lake was formed from an old swamp. In a sense, Frederic was creating another landscape to paint with the Hudson River and Catskills as a backdrop. During this period, Isabel gave birth to two children who both tragically died from diphtheria in 1865. In 1867, Frederic was able to purchase an additional 18 acres at the top of the hill which overlooked his farm, and decided to build a more substantial house there. That same year, Isabel and Frederic traveled for 18 months in Europe, the Middle East, Beirut and Israel, and these travels became the inspiration for the new house to be built at the top of the hill. From 1866 to 1871, they had four more children, and in 1872, the family moved into their new house, although it was not finished until two years later. The house was designed largely by Frederic with the help of Calvert Vaux - Olmsted's partner in the creation of Central Park - and was inspired by the architecture observed on his visit to the Middle East. He was involved not only with the structural design, but also with the decorative details of the house. At the same time, he continued to run the farm and refine the landscape with careful attention to the placement of roads, trees and fields.

Olana was the Churchs's primary residence from the 1870's until his death in 1900. He continued to paint, but his output was reduced because he developed rheumatoid arthritis. His son, Louis and Louis's wife, Sally, inherited the estate and lived there until Sally's death in 1964. At that time, Sally's heirs inherited the entire estate and prepared the estate for sale. Due to the interest of a Smith College Art Professor who marshalled the energy of the community as well as prominent New Yorkers, a fund raising effort was undertaken to raise $470,000 needed to purchase the land, house and house contents. The estate was saved, and in 1966, and it was made a New York State Historic Site.

The grounds are open year round. During the summer the house is open Tuesday through Sunday, and in the winter months there is a more limited schedule (check website).The house can be viewed only with a guided tour, and these tours are very popular so advance registration is suggested. The contents of the house are original to Church's time, and the house is filled with his paintings as well as works by other artists including those of Thomas Cole, his mentor. Treasures collected on his travels are also exhibited in the house. From the house's site on top of a hill, the views of the Hudson and the Catskills beyond and the farm below are what you might expect in one of Church's paintings. The grounds, also designed by Church, can be viewed on foot or by a touring vehicle. There is a small garden near the house. However, it is Church's arrangement of trees, fields and pathways which create a breathtaking landscape.

Olana

ACKNOWLEDGEMENTS

Writing this guidebook has been a terrific experience and an opportunity to brush up on American history, architecture, landscape architecture and the beautiful geography of New England. A number of people have guided me through this process as well as supported me in what started as a quixotic dream:

- Foremost, is my wife Cynthia who edited the book, as well as tolerated being awakened from a midnight sleep to hear my latest inspiration.
- John Peranzi, an aspiring Brown medical student, who not only raked my lawn, but essentially typed the entire book and guided me through my anxieties and crises with the computer.
- Kathy Bell, librarian at Tower Hill Botanical Garden, who took the time to research previous books and gardens and convinced me that there were no good guidebooks on historic houses and gardens.
- Karen Binder, executive director at Blithewold, who was excited about the concept of a guidebook and was not afraid to give me constructive feedback.
- Margaret Whitehead, archivist at Blithewold, who encouraged me to consider self-publishing, and shared her positive experiences doing the same.
- Bill Noble, who gave me my first list of houses and gardens to see, as well as the names of people in the field to contact.

- My brother, Charles, the former executive editor of Sail Magazine, who was very supportive of a long shot and went the extra mile to track down information regarding publishing companies.
- Bob Whitcomb, the former editor of the Providence Journal, who took the time to patiently walk me through the steps of writing and publishing a book.
- The individuals at each site that took the time to wade through my summaries and correct my inaccuracies as well as to provide me with photographs.
- Alexa Terfloth, a recent RISD graduate in graphic arts who patiently worked with me to develop maps which would lend a geographic context to all the houses and gardens.
- The folks at I-Universe for their professionalism, efficiency, flexibility, and their willingness to walk me through the mogul fields faced by a novice author.

Printed in the United States
by Baker & Taylor Publisher Services